men and women

HUMAN BEHAVIOR

men and women

BY PETER SWERDLOFF
AND THE EDITORS OF TIME-LIFE BOOKS

TIME-LIFE BOOKS, NEW YORK

The Author: Peter Swerdloff is a freelance writer who was formerly a member of the staff of Time and prior to that, *Newsweek*. A resident of New York City, Mr. Swerdloff has written articles for a number of other periodicals, including Fortune and *Esquire*.

General Consultants for Human Behavior:
Robert M. Krauss is Professor of Psychology at Columbia University. He has taught at Princeton and Harvard and was Chairman of the Psychology Department at Rutgers. He is the co-author of *Theories in Social Psychology*, edits the *Journal of Experimental Social Psychology* and contributes articles to many journals on aspects of human behavior and social interaction.

Peter I. Rose, a specialist on racial and ethnic relations, is Sophia Smith Professor of Sociology and Anthropology at Smith College and is on the graduate faculty of the University of Massachusetts. His books include *They and We, The Subject Is Race* and *Americans from Africa*. Professor Rose has also taught at Goucher, Wesleyan, Colorado, Clark, Yale, Amherst, the University of Leicester in England, Kyoto University in Japan and Flinders University in Australia.

James W. Fernandez is Chairman of the Anthropology Department at Dartmouth College. His research in culture change has taken him to East, West and South Africa and the Iberian peninsula. Articles on his field studies have been widely published in European and American anthropology journals. He has been president of the Northeastern Anthropological Association and a consultant to the Foreign Service Institute.

Special Consultant for Men and Women:
Philip Shaver, Assistant Professor of Psychology at Columbia University, has published articles on sex differences and sex roles in *The Journal of Personality and Social Psychology* and the *Journal of Educational Psychology*. He is a member of the editorial boards of *Behavioral Science* and the *Journal of Experimental Social Psychology*.

Contents

Dominion of the Male

1

Oddly enough, sex is one of nature's afterthoughts. For better than two thirds of the earth's existence, living things got along quite satisfactorily even though every species existed in only one basic form instead of being differentiated into two distinct sexes. Simple creatures reproduced by splitting in two, leaving two offspring where there had been one parent. Complicated things grew buds, or sent out shoots or limbs that developed into independent creatures.

But there are limits to the complexity of life forms that can split in two; a sea squirt is about the most complicated living thing that can reproduce by dividing. Instead of requiring the division of intricate cells, organs and structures, sexual reproduction transmits, through the chromosomes and genes of the male and female, a kind of map or blueprint for new members of a species to follow. The new members grow their own complex bodies, assembling simple materials according to the plan that they inherited. In this way complicated results are feasible. It was sex that made possible the evolution of such complex and diverse creatures as dinosaurs, eagles, whales—and human beings—where only fungi and algae and amoebae had earlier prevailed.

If there are sexes, each must have its own unique role in reproduction. And sexual specialization almost invariably leads to a division of function that extends beyond the realm of reproduction. In most living things certain activities, along with certain traits, are characteristic of one sex but not of the other, and the two sexes nearly always stand in a particular relationship to each other. Generally the females of the species take care of the young and the nest on the homesite, if there is one, and while the males may help to feed the young, they are more or less free agents.

In human beings this division of responsibilities has been exaggerated into a unique relationship between the sexes. Men have come to be considered the dominant sex. Women must remain several steps behind —literally in such countries as Morocco *(left)*, figuratively almost everywhere else. "This world has always belonged to the men," wrote the French author Simone de Beauvoir. Not many knowledgeable people doubt that she is right. "All contemporary societies, whatever their kinship organization or mode of subsistence, are characterized by some degree of male dominance," asserted anthropologists Michelle Rosaldo and Louise Lamphere. "Sexual asymmetry is presently a universal fact of human social life."

Once upon a time this imbalance was widely accepted as inevitable and even just. The differences between men and women, their roles, the whole complex relationship between the sexes, all were taken for granted. It was understood that men are assertive and strong, women submissive and weak, that men are born to fight, to provide and to build, women to bear children and to act as companions and servants of men. Now, the differences, the roles and the relationship are all under challenge as never before.

The challenge springs from two sources. One is the accumulating body of scientific knowledge about the differences between the sexes. In recent years scientists have demonstrated that innate biological differrences between males and females are few indeed. There is no physical reason why women cannot compose great symphonies, manage banks or drive buses—or why men cannot take care of babies, nurse sick people or type letters. Thus the differences in what men and women generally do seems not to depend on the way men and women are made. And yet in some very special instances it may.

The latest studies of the sexes also suggest that biology may influence behavior more than some people would like to believe. The results of some experiments contain tantalizing hints that men and women may perceive the world in different ways, while other studies point to the fact that hormones secreted before and after birth may affect an individual's interests, emotions and such important human traits as aggressiveness. How much of this behavior is truly biological—innate and unchangeable—and how much of it is learned, an artificial expression of cultural tradition, is a puzzle that will not be sorted out for many generations to come. For the overwhelming power of society's teachings to mold behavior is only now being fully appreciated. From this new understanding comes the second important challenge to the tradition of male dominance.

By analyzing the activities of peoples in different parts of the world and at different periods of history, scholars have discovered that the roles of men and women shift back and forth from time to time and place to place. Women can be regarded as slaves or as valued leaders.

Men may take to themselves the duties of child care, and women may do battle in war. This evidence demonstrates that many traditional masculine and feminine roles are not inherited but are learned from the culture in which a human being grows up. As a result, it is now undisputed that roles once thought immutable can change from generation to generation and even within one generation. If the roles are artificial, so too is the traditional dominance of men.

Even before the dawn of history, scientists believe, man became the ruler of the roost, establishing the design for living that generally prevails today. Everywhere, even if women are highly regarded, the activities of men are valued more than those of women. It matters not a whit how a society allocates roles and tasks between the sexes; those that belong to men inevitably count for more in the eyes of the whole community. In societies where men fish and women do beadwork, fishing brings greater prestige; where women fish and men work with beads, it is beadwork that matters. Similarly, there are parts of New Guinea where women cultivate sweet potatoes and men, yams. The two foods are similar and yet, reports Michelle Rosaldo, "Yams are the prestige food, the food one distributes at feasts." In the same way, ordinary cooking is the job of women in most societies and is little valued, while grande cuisine is the prestige work of honored male chefs. "The second sex," women have been called, or "the subordinate sex."

It is not hard to find evidence in every age of male disdain for women and of female subjection to men. Ancient Bedouin maintained that women were made of monkey's tails, or else of the sins of the satans. The Zulus thanked the gods for the birth of a boy by slaughtering an ox but could not be bothered when the new child was a girl; after all, they said, "She is merely a weed."

In ancient Athens and Rome a woman remained essentially a minor as long as she lived. In medieval Europe she could own no property, she was frequently married off against her will, she could not divorce her husband, and if she committed adultery, she was sometimes put to death. (An adulterous husband went free.) Even in the more enlightened 18th and 19th centuries, the common law of England and the United States held that a woman, like a felon committed to prison, lost most of her civil rights when she entered into marriage. She could neither sign papers nor testify in court. She was not permitted to manage property even if she owned it, and she was not entitled to keep possession of either her earnings or her children if her husband chose to take them away. Sir William Blackstone summed up a wife's legal sta-

The traditional roles of the sexes are learned at such an early age that very young children often seem to be giving precocious imitations of the behavior of men and women. At left, a girl in Helsinki, Finland, has already learned how to sashay enticingly past a boy of about the same age. And he, in turn, is already adept at girl-watching.

tus in his *Commentaries on the Laws of England* of 1765-69: "The very being or legal existence of the woman is suspended . . . or at least is incorporated and consolidated into that of the husband." In France that apostle of egalitarianism, Jean Jacques Rousseau, said, "Women have, or ought to have, but little liberty." And as recently as World War I, a well-bred Englishman announced the birth of his daughter by asking a friend, "Have you heard of our fiasco?"

No one is sure how this notion of male superiority arose, but scientists have advanced two possible explanations. One is based on a fact —that males are generally stronger than females. The other is based on a feeling—that women are closer to nature than men.

According to the first explanation, men began to lord it over women because their physical strength was crucial to survival in early societies and thus made men seem more valuable than women. Men could run faster and farther than women in pursuit of game for food. They were better than women at clubbing wild beasts or human marauders. The generally lesser strength of females was reduced still more by the demands of menstruation, pregnancy and childbirth; much of the time, women had to depend on men to bring them enough to eat and to protect them against the dangers of primitive life.

There is a remarkable paradox in the prestige of power granted men because of their strength. Although they have consigned females to second-class citizenship because of their lack of strength, men have also been perfectly willing—eager, in fact—to impose backbreaking tasks on the physically weaker sex *(pages 14-15)*. In nomadic tribes, women serve as beasts of burden and from the beginning of agriculture (probably invented by women), they have done much of the plowing, harvesting and other strenuous farm chores.

The English Classical scholar Margaret Hasluck studied pastoral Balkan societies during the 1930s and found that when an Albanian family had only one donkey, it was the man who rode while the woman walked behind, often carrying loads weighing as much as 70 pounds. John K. Campbell, an English anthropologist, found in Greece that Sarakatsani males did condescend to lift heavy burdens so they could be tied to a mule, but they never carried anything on their own backs. "However sick or feeble his wife or daughter, a man will never help her with the intolerable burden of heavy water barrels," Campbell observed. In the modern technological world, a man is likely to display somewhat more gallantry toward women. However, he rarely uses his own brawn. Ordinarily he reserves to himself the physically easier work of government, religion, supervision and general pencil-pushing. The housewife

plus qe li uenurs car trop aen urz me   depart ceuos. O)es piuz qe qe uor qe
                                                          feir licomenr. fi me rezonere.·.

who balances a 10-month-old on her hip dozens of times a day, lugs gro-
ceries and carries the 20-pound vacuum cleaner up the stairs expends
more muscle power in an average day than her husband would use while
working at his desk in the office.

As a practical matter, the superior strength of the male obviously cannot explain male dominance in today's world even though it was
undoubtedly an important factor in establishing the habit of dominance
by men. An equally important—and more complicated—explanation
for the relative status of men and women has been suggested by the
French anthropologist Claude Lévi-Strauss and others. This theory iden-
tifies women with inferior nature, men with superior culture. Women,
the theory holds, are often perceived as being closer to nature than men
because their bodies tie them closely to earthy functions like menstruation, childbirth and lactation. The woman's animality is thus more apparent than the man's, and, as anthropologist Michelle Rosaldo of
Stanford University explains, "Women are more involved than men in

The stereotype of the brave man and fragile woman was romanticized in depictions of knighthood such as this illustration from a 14th Century manuscript. Exemplifying the stories that have shaped Western behavior for centuries, the manuscript shows stern knights riding off to combat, while their ladies stay behind to run the castle and glorify the men's deeds in tapestries.

the 'grubby' and dangerous stuff of social existence, giving birth and mourning death, feeding, cooking, disposing of feces, and the like."

By contrast, men are often identified with culture, with human consciousness and its achievements, in short, with the lofty realm of life that transcends nature. The human male, Simone de Beauvoir says, "remodels the face of the earth, he creates new instruments, he invents, he shapes the future." As a result, says anthropologist Sherry Ortner, he assumes the dominant role. "Culture at some level of awareness asserts itself to be not only distinct from but superior to nature . . . if women were considered part of nature, then culture would find it 'natural' to subordinate, not to say oppress, them."

Surprisingly enough, the female's tie with nature has been used as an excuse not only to diminish but also to exalt her. The second is not much better than the first; both ways of looking at women deny them equality with men. In early agricultural societies, as in certain surviving Australian, Indian and Polynesian tribes, the female capacity to bear children led males to believe that women possessed a magical power to make crops grow and therefore to keep the community alive. In Japan from the Third to the Eighth centuries, there were numerous sorcerer-queens who ruled less as women than as special beings valued from afar because it was believed that they knew how to control supernatural forces. In 19th Century Europe the Victorian notion of women as purity incarnate was not really so very different—and it was just as useful for keeping the women in their place. This belief, said Bertrand Russell, "was part and parcel of the determination to keep them inferior politically and economically."

If men have always enjoyed the major share of human power, women have sometimes won a share nearly as big. There may never have been a true matriarchy, a society ruled by females. And it is certain that the Amazons never existed (although the myth seems based on real people, the Sarmatians of Fourth Century B.C. Russia, who drafted unmarried women into their fighting troops).

Yet there have been a few cultures in which women commanded respect and wielded considerable power. They tell something about future possibilities for sexual equality, for they demonstrate that the status of females is culturally determined rather than given in the nature of things. And they provide hints about factors that promote equality. While anthropologists admit that they cannot yet explain why women do better in some societies than in others, some conditions appear to favor equality. In some cases, at least, female status is higher than usual when the social climate is generally stable and liberal, when men are

A woman construction worker trundles a wheelbarrow down a Moscow street. Women fill one out of every three jobs in the Soviet construction industry.

Heavy labor for the "weaker" sex

As a matter of biological fact, men generally surpass women in stature and strength. But a fact can be misleading. Far from behaving like the weaker sex, women can and do perform much of the hard work of the world.

Some of that work arises in woman's traditional role as homemaker. But custom or necessity also assigns to women heavy labor in both industrial and agricultural societies. In the Soviet Union women fill almost half the factory jobs and over two fifths of the jobs on farms. In Japanese fishing villages, while the men put out to sea, women raise crops and process the fishermen's catch. And in the mountain villages of Albania a woman may often serve as beast of burden: if her family cannot afford a donkey, the woman of the house will carry 70-pound loads of firewood from an outlying wood lot to her home.

In an Italian mountain village, laundry day calls for a backbreaking routine of pounding, scrubbing and rinsing on the bank of a running stream.

While their men work at a nearby factory, these Bulgarian women cultivate rows of cauliflower. After a long day in the field they will head home to cook dinner.

Two women of central Java help bring in the rice crop. In rural Indonesian cultures men and women share the work, from field labor to household chores.

A Spanish peasant girl deftly balances a tray of bread dough on its way to the communal oven. The 24 loaves are a week's ration for a family of eight.

Having wrestled a ewe to the ground, a Cretan sheepshearer pins it firmly as she goes about her job. A master of her craft, she can shear four animals an hour.

often away from home waging war or for other purposes, when women produce a large share of the food supply, when they have control over salable products, when they organize themselves into what one anthropologist calls "female solidarity groups," and when men take a major part in bringing up the children.

In ancient Egypt, when the prevailing temper of the times was rather liberal, women enjoyed considerable independence, enough to attract the attention of Greek travelers like the historian Herodotus. Some Egyptian women, he reported, followed trades or worked for pay. Also the first wife in a polygamous home enjoyed considerable legal protection. A woman could marry whom she pleased, and when she did, she became half-owner of her husband's property. Under certain circumstances it was also possible for her to divorce him, while at the same time, a prenuptial contract protected her against capricious divorce by her husband. Furthermore, when a couple did separate, the husband generally returned his wife's dowry.

In Sparta, alone among the Greek cities, women were very nearly equal to men. For one thing, males were often away fighting military engagements; in their absence, women were allowed to manage and even to own land. Perhaps more important, Sparta rejected the institution of the family in favor of the commune. All of the children belonged to the city as a whole, and in order to breed offspring for the benefit of the entire community the exchange of husbands and wives was acceptable. As a result, the concept of adultery disappeared, and no man and woman were bound to each other. Apart from the obligation to have children, Spartan women were free agents. Men and women competed against each other in athletic contests, including wrestling matches, and they participated jointly in parades and public dances. Even when it came to politics and government affairs, equality prevailed because the women had as much say as the men.

A quite different kind of society in which at least some women held high status was, surprisingly, Japan. Today this country has a tradition of female subservience, but between the 10th and 16th centuries the opposite was true. The women of the Japanese aristocracy then rejoiced in freedom and power seldom known elsewhere. Classics of Japanese literature were the work of women: Murasaki Shikibu, a daughter of the powerful Fujiwara clan, wrote an evocative novel of court life called *The Tale of Genji,* and her rival in belles lettres, Sei Shonagon, produced *Pillow Book,* a nonfiction collection of witty puns and lyrical descriptions of court life.

Even more remarkable was the military role of women. When the samurai, or warrior aristocracy, emerged during the 13th Century, a few women became legendary fighters and were immortalized in the popular Kamakura war tales. The black-haired, fair-skinned Tomoe, for example, was said to be "a match for a thousand warriors and fit to meet either God or devil." More than once, it was recorded, she had "taken the field, armed at all points, and won matchless renown in encounters with the bravest captains." In one fight, "when all the others had been slain or had fled, among the last seven there rode Tomoe." This golden age for some Japanese women ended when the country descended into feudalism and the government was unable to protect property; landowners willed their estates to the single son strong enough to hold onto it, disinheriting daughters.

Less spectacular but perhaps more significant was the influence exerted by women among the Iroquois Indians of North America. At one time, a few observers thought that Iroquois females were more powerful than males. That judgment is no longer considered correct, but anthropologist George Murdock says that the Iroquois "of all the people of the earth approach most closely to that hypothetical form of society known as the matriarchate."

Among these Indians the division of labor ran along traditional lines. The men were often away from home waging war or trading. And they also assumed the usual male tasks of putting up the palisades that protected each village against intruders, building the long houses jointly occupied by several families, hunting and fishing, building canoes, paddles and other equipment, as well as clearing land for farming and harvesting the crops. The women, too, held to "women's work,"—homemaking and gardening—but with significant departures from tradition. Working in gangs, which were bossed by a member of the other sex, they grew corn, beans and squash, and gathered wild vegetables. Altogether, women provided about half of the community's food supply, and they controlled their share of it through a kind of female mutual-aid society.

More unusual than these aspects of Iroquois woman-power was the female role in government. The Iroquois women exerted great influence at three main levels; the clan council, representing all the families who belonged to a single clan; the tribal council, made up of delegates from member clans; and the council of the Iroquois League, which was composed of five tribes. Influential older women served as electors for all these bodies, nominating younger relatives for membership on them, issuing public warnings to members who neglected their constituents' interests and beginning impeachment proceedings against those who displeased them. Older women also influenced tribal affairs on occasion by withholding food supplies from certain war parties. But in every instance, council members and chieftains were male, and ultimate power was invariably wielded by men. The noted anthropologist Margaret Mead suggests that the women's influence was based less on their sex than on their age: "When examined closely the situation there resolved itself into the dominance of the elder members of the kin group over the younger males."

A similar status is held today by women in many tribes that follow ancient patterns of behavior. In Africa, Yoruba women must pretend to be ignorant and acquiescent in the presence of their husbands, and when serving meals, they are required to kneel at their husbands' feet. Yet these same women are the most independent members of their sex in Africa and they command considerable economic power. Most of it comes from their role as traders. The Yoruba women buy cocoa, yams and corn —crops raised by men—for resale in distant markets. They also deal in works of art, mostly bronze statues and carvings of wood, bone and ivory done by men, along with baskets, mats and pottery fashioned by women. All of the cash that they realize from these commercial ventures is theirs to manage. To protect their economic interests, they have set up trade guilds that set standards for the women's crafts. Through the guilds, the women exert some control over political affairs, although Yoruba leaders are always men.

In the Philippines, Ilongot men and women come fairly close to equality in status. Some males win special recognition for a men-only activity, head-hunting. And all able-bodied males gain status from hunting animals, a pursuit that Ilongot society rates higher than the farming done by females. Nevertheless hunting and gardening are seen as complementary ways of obtaining food, and at mealtimes men cook and serve the game they have shot, while women prepare and serve their vegetables. Most important, according to anthropologist Michelle Rosaldo, is the fact that while wives spend long hours tending their gardens, husbands look after the children. The result is a more or less egalitarian relationship between the sexes, at least at home. "When a man is involved in domestic labor, in child care and cooking, he cannot establish an aura of authority and distance," Rosaldo believes.

Such examples of woman-power are notable just because there are so few of them. Only in isolated places or isolated times has there been anything approaching equality between the sexes. The strictures of biology generally outweighed all other considerations; male strength and fe-

As portrayed by 19th Century actress Elizabeth Crocker Bowers, Lady Macbeth is an almost terrifying figure. In a first-act soliloquy (left) she renounces her womanhood as she plans to spur Macbeth on to murder. "Unsex me here," she cries, "and fill me, from the crown to the toe, top-full of direst cruelty!"

The wily woman behind the scenes

In a world dominated by men, many strong-minded women have acquired power by dominating their men—often with significant consequences. A courtesan named Theodora became wife and co-ruler to the Byzantine emperor Justinian; in 532 A.D. she saved his throne by persuading him to defend his capital against rioting mobs. Eleanor of Aquitaine influenced the destiny of two nations—first as queen to French king Louis VII (she accompanied him on the Second Crusade); later as queen to the English king Henry II (she helped administer his kingdom).

With less official authority but no less power, Madame de Pompadour, mistress to King Louis XV of France, took a hand in foreign policy and sponsored the building of the Petit Trianon at Versailles. But perhaps the most famous of such women was more a fictional than a historical character—Shakespeare's Lady Macbeth *(left)*, who set her husband on the path to the Scottish throne and induced him to murder the reigning King Duncan.

male childbearing were in full-time demand simply for survival of the species. The possibility of broad equality did not appear until those limitations were lifted by the industrial and medical revolutions of the 18th and 19th centuries.

When machines began to take over the hard work formerly done by men, male physical strength counted for less. Equally important, industry increased women's freedom as more and more wives went outside their homes to seek jobs. Women began to see the world and the possibilities it offered them in a new way.

Eventually, their widened horizons and their increased economic power brought wives into a new relationship with their husbands. With wives more and more occupied outside the family, at least some men have begun to help with the children, and spurred by the invention of labor-saving devices that made traditional "women's work" seem less feminine, men also are more willing to accept some household chores. Gradually the balance of family power has shifted. In a study of 731 households in Detroit, Michigan, sociologists Robert Blood and D. M. Wolfe discovered that "a working wife's husband listens to her more, and she listens to herself more. She expresses herself and has more opinions. Instead of looking up into her husband's eyes and worshipping him, she levels with him, compromising on the issues at hand. Thus her power increases and the husband's falls."

Medical advances were perhaps even more liberating than the Industrial Revoluiton. Between 1900 and 1975, infant mortality in the United States and most of Western Europe decreased from over 200 per thousand to 30 per thousand. Consequently, as the French minister of women's affairs Françoise Giroud has noted, "To have three living children, all a woman has to do is have three children—instead of six or seven or eight." Many wives these days are through with childbearing by age 25, and with improved life expectancy (up from 48 in 1900 to 77 in 1975) they have decades of good health and energy ahead of them. The more recent introduction of simple and reliable contraception has equally pervasive consequences. Freed from the necessity of bearing extra or unwanted children, women can plan productive lives outside the home. Not only can they find jobs or look for other ways in which to use their talents, but also they can commit themselves to specialized training with the confidence that long-term, satisfying careers are practical objectives.

If the industrial and medical revolutions made increased freedom for women a possibility, what made it a reality was the women's rights movement. For just as the status of blacks all over the world remained little improved until blacks themselves began pushing for improvement, so the position of women did not change much until they themselves began insisting that it had to.

The organized drive for women's equality came in two waves, the first beginning during the second quarter of the 19th Century, the other getting under way in the 1960s, although of course its origins can be found earlier. The first significant brief for the female sex, a book called *Vindication of the Rights of Woman,* was published in 1792 by Mary Wollstonecraft. This beautiful Englishwoman mounted no attack on men (she loved several) or on marriage (she was happiest as wife and mother). All she wanted, she wrote, was "to see women neither heroines nor brutes; but reasonable creatures." She believed they deserved a sound education and the right to work for a living if they wanted to. Aston-

The personification of male supremacy, Henry VIII almost seems to gloat from this Holbein portrait. The Tudor king viewed women merely as instruments of his will and summarily disposed of them when they were no longer useful. He divorced two wives and had two executed. In 16th Century England, where women had few rights, the fate of Henry's helpmeets was readily accepted.

ANNO · ÆTATIS ·   · SVÆ · XLIX ·

Women who made it in a man's world

Through most of history, it took an exceptional set of circumstances to propel a woman to power, and an exceptional woman to make a lasting mark in a man's world. Among the select few who beat the odds, the four at right are perhaps the most famous.

Each of these women achieved a position of great power, and each made an indelible impression on the history of her country. They were strikingly different in some ways. One was a seductress and one a spinster, one a mystic and one a usurper. But they shared key attributes. Each was exceptionally shrewd and single-minded, and each showed by her achievements she was as adept with power as any man.

Cleopatra skillfully used her allure to forestall her country's absorption into the Roman Empire for 20 years. The religiously motivated Joan of Arc led France's soldiers to victory against a hated enemy, the British. Catherine the Great seized the throne of Russia, then presided over the nation's expansion into one of the world's great powers. And Elizabeth I of England, who never married, brilliantly nursed and bullied her country into perhaps the greatest era in its history.

France's peasant-warrior, Joan of Arc, attends the coronation of King Charles at Rheims Cathedral. She heard voices calling her to her country's service, and led an army to victory over the British.

Egypt's languorous queen, Cleopatra, traveled by barge to a rendezvous with Mark Antony (center). By beguiling him —and his predecessor, Julius Caesar— she preserved her country's independence. But when a third would-be conqueror, Octavian, spurned her she killed herself, and Egypt was annexed by Rome.

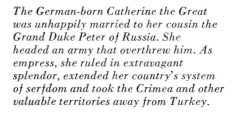

Elizabeth I surrounded herself with able men, and played off marriage proposals from the princes of Europe for 25 years, never accepting any. A brilliant and resourceful ruler, she presided over the defeat of the Spanish Armada, made peace at home and abroad and raised her country to the front rank of nations.

The German-born Catherine the Great was unhappily married to her cousin the Grand Duke Peter of Russia. She headed an army that overthrew him. As empress, she ruled in extravagant splendor, extended her country's system of serfdom and took the Crimea and other valuable territories away from Turkey.

ishingly at that period in history, she managed to live the life that she advocated. She supported herself by writing, traveled abroad, lived for a while in an apartment of her own and was accepted as an intellectual equal at dinner parties where the other guests were men like the chemist Joseph Priestly, the painter Henry Fuseli and the hero of the American and French revolutions, Thomas Paine.

In the decades that followed publication of Mary Wollstonecraft's book, feminists became increasingly numerous, vocal and effective. In the United States, for example, the sisters Sarah and Angelina Grimké from South Carolina were among those early liberationists who were pressing for reform. An 1838 essay by Sarah Grimké proclaimed "that intellect is not sexed; that strength of mind is not sexed; and that our views about the duties of man . . . and the duties of women, the spheres of man and the spheres of women are merely arbitrary opinions, differing in different ages and countries, and dependent solely on the will and judgment of erring mortals."

Besides Sarah and Angelina Grimké, some of the most influential American activists in the 19th Century struggle for women's rights were Elizabeth Cady Stanton, Susan B. Anthony and Amelia Jenks Bloomer. "Would to God you could know the burning indignation that fills a woman's soul when she sees how like feudal barons you free men hold your women," Mrs. Stanton said once in a speech to the New York State legislature. It was Elizabeth Stanton, along with several other feminists, who issued a call for the first convention ever held to discuss the rights of the female sex. Meeting in 1848 in Seneca Falls, New York, 68 women and 32 men signed a declaration of principles drafted by Mrs. Stanton. "We hold these truths to be self-evident: that all men and women are created equal," the declaration began. "The history of mankind," it continued, "is a history of repeated injuries and usurpations on the part of man toward woman, having in direct object the establishment of an absolute tyranny over her."

One of Mrs. Stanton's closest friends was Susan B. Anthony. A teacher for 15 years, Mrs. Anthony began her career as a champion of women's rights by demanding that teachers of both sexes get the same pay. Before she decided to center her efforts on winning the ballot, she also advocated greater equality between husbands and wives at home. "It may be delayed longer than we think; it may be here sooner than we expect; but the day will come when man will recognize woman as his peer, not only at the fireside but in the councils of the nation. Then, and not until then, will there be perfect comradeship, the ideal union between the sexes," Mrs. Anthony wrote.

Mrs. Bloomer, of course, was a sartorial pacesetter as well as a suffragette. The very name conjures up a hilarious picture of loose trousers gathered tightly at the ankle and worn under a full, calf-length skirt. The costume was Mrs. Bloomer's idea of dress reform, and like Mrs. Stanton, Mrs. Anthony and other leading feminists, she wore bloomers for some time, enduring the hoots and jeers of all those—and there were many—who thought the outfit looked ridiculous and, worse yet, symbolized radicalism. "The Bloomer girls," as they came to be known, were smart enough to realize that their costume was alienating possible supporters, and eventually they went back to dressing like other women. Mrs. Bloomer wanted to reform much more than dress. In 1849 she started a magazine called *Lily*, believed to be the first publication edited by a woman. In its pages she advocated temperance along with women's suffrage and other feminist rights.

In Britain, the feminist movement got underway in 1867 when philosopher John Stuart Mill asked Parliament to grant women the franchise (he lost 73-196). To dramatize the long battle for suffrage, Emmeline Pankhurst founded the Women's Social and Political Union in 1903. At first nonviolent, its members began in 1912 to interrupt speeches in Parliament, trample public flower gardens, invade the British Museum and the Tower of London, hurl stones at police officers and even burn houses. One suffragette, Emily Wilding Davison, threw herself in front of the King's own horse at the 1913 Derby and was fatally injured. Another, Lady Constance Lytton, arrested during a street demonstration, suffered from heart trouble but she disdained to use her rank as a way of getting preferential treatment. Telling the police that she was Jane Warton, a seamstress, she was force-fed when she went on a hunger strike in jail.

Women's liberation reached a kind of apogee at the time of World War I. It was then that women shared the concerns of men as they never had before and got a chance to show what they could do in home-front jobs once considered suitable for men only. In 1920, the 19th Amendment to the United States Constitution guaranteed women the right to vote—long after they had already won that right in many European countries. But the franchise was not granted in Britain until 1928 (and not until after World War II in Japan).

The drive for equality subsided after the vote was won. Partly it was overshadowed by the concerns of the Great Depression of the 1930s, quickly followed by the horrors of World War II. But partly the feminists' efforts slowed from an illusion of victory. It took women many

years to realize what blacks, too, came to understand: that getting the right to vote does not automatically bring full citizenship or genuine equality. As historian William O'Neill observed, "The ballot did not materially help women . . . to better themselves or improve their status." They still had trouble finding good jobs, winning promotions, achieving recognition for their accomplishments and earning the respect due them as men's equals.

A second wave of feminism was therefore inevitable. It did not rise up until the 1960s. Once more, the center of activity was the United States, perhaps because American women already had so much more freedom and affluence than women elsewhere in the world that they dared to hope for even more. A number of books and articles—prominent among them *The Feminine Mystique* by Betty Friedan—brought to the surface the dissatisfaction that was felt by women across the country. A group of determined, resourceful leaders of the women's liberation movement—Friedan, Shirley Chisholm, Kate Millett, Gloria Steinem and Martha Griffiths—drew support from men as well as women for drastic changes in American life.

Outside the United States, the new feminism has had trouble not only in finding leaders but also in mobilizing followers. In Italy, top feminists are referred to as "the generals without an army." Where liberationists are active in Europe and Asia, their goals—the right to abortion, more day care centers, equal pay for equal work, and similar objectives—have been less sweeping than those of American reformers and their style quieter, freer of the hostility toward men that American militants often display. "The battle is not taken into the bedroom here," says the French author Ingrid Carlander.

But everywhere the times were right for change. Industrialization had reached into almost all parts of the globe. So had modern medicine's promise of easy contraception and healthy lives for wanted children. Perhaps because of these powerful forces, but perhaps for completely unrelated reasons, styles of living have altered drastically in a world where hardly anyone could continue traditional ways in isolation, free of outside influence.

One indicator of change is that child-rearing practices have become much different than they used to be. Psychologist Urie Bronfenbrenner believes that over the past half century, middle-class parents have more and more tended to bring up both girls and boys in about the same way instead of making rigid distinctions between the sexes. And sociologist Robert Blood is convinced that "the roles of men and women are converging for both adults and children."

The convergence of roles has become more and more apparent over the past decade, in Europe, in the United States and, to a lesser extent, in most other parts of the world. The feminist struggle has brought about changes in both behavior and attitudes. The law gives increasing recognition to the idea that men and women are equal. Business, industry and the professions are making it easier for women to take their rightful places beside men, entering new fields and moving ahead in old ones. Book publishers and educational institutions are taking steps to eliminate sexism from their textbooks and their curricula. Men are examining old prejudices and relinquishing old privileges. But it has become obvious that not all of the differences between the sexes can ever be completely eliminated—if indeed, anyone would want to eliminate them—for to some extent the relationships between the sexes are fixed by unalterable facts of biology.

27

Demanding more of marriage

The most enduring and intimate relationship between man and woman is formalized in an institution older than recorded history: marriage. But in recent decades increased pressures on this arrangement have challenged the institution itself. This seems especially true in Scandinavia and the United States. Young people approach marriage more warily. Many find alternatives. In the U.S. the average age of those who do marry has gone up almost a year within the past two decades, after a steady decline in this century.

Behind such statistics lie changes in attitudes toward marriage. People expect more of it than ever, are more readily disillusioned when it does not meet expectations, and refuse to accept its failures uncomplainingly *(right)*.

Marriage used to be relatively simple. A young man exchanged vows with a neighbor's daughter—often by agreement between the parents. He got a childbearer and cook-housekeeper, she got a breadwinner. Neither expected much more. But today, education, affluence and leisure have radically altered the attitudes of both wife and husband. Now each expects the other to play a multiplicity of roles, filling needs beyond those of housework and economic support. Each of the partners must be an expert lover, an efficient co-worker, a source of emotional support and a rewarding companion.

Demanding as all these roles may be, the hope of combining them successfully still makes marriage so appealing that most people do get married. And —in the United States at least—four out of five persons whose first marriages do not work care enough about the institution to try again.

Agreeing to disagree, a couple in Bottrop, Germany, ends a spat about money the wife has spent. In the new marriages, such quarrels are less threatening, offering as they do a way to strengthen a union through honest expression.

A new premium on sex appeal

Today's couples, coming of age in the emancipated atmosphere of the sexual revolution, expect more physical gratification from each other than earlier generations did. They know more about sex, for they have grown up at a time when sex manuals have glutted the market. In the early 1970s, for example, *The Joy of Sex* by the English scientist Alex Comfort, sold millions of copies around the world.

Modern youngsters may also be more experienced sexually than were their parents, partly because improved contraceptives help eliminate the risk of pregnancy from sexual relations. In Sweden, one study found that 93 per cent of engaged couples have premarital sexual relations. Contraceptives are also an important factor in married couples' more frequent sexual activity—up 21 per cent in the United States, according to a 1974 survey.

But the most striking innovation in married sex has been brought about primarily by changing feminine attitudes. Women, who once were taught to view intercourse as a burden, now expect the physical fulfillment that previously was considered a male prerogative. Says one marriage counselor, "Women are much less satisfied not to have orgasms than they used to be." Sexologists William Masters and Virginia Johnson point out the benefits of sexual equality: for the man less fear of inadequate performance, for the woman freedom to participate as a partner. "The potential rewards from parity of sexual roles," they write, "are limitless."

Pausing to flirt, a girl on a street in Torremolinos, Spain, flashes a smile at two friendly young men. Only a few years ago, such a sexually liberated encounter was unthinkable in Spain, where young women rarely went out alone, and men were deeply shocked by enticing behavior.

In England, where sexual permissiveness has replaced the repression that was the rule of Victorian times, lovers embrace at a beach.

Two-way help in time of need

During most of human history, when three or four generations lived under the same roof from cradle to grave, a couple beset by crisis found ready support from relatives. Today, husbands and wives frequently have only each other to count on in times of need—up to and including childbirth *(right)*.

In mobile America, where each year one fifth of all families move to a different home, even neighbors may be strangers. According to the Family Service Association of America, the largest counseling agency in the nation, the most important element in ensuring the survival of a marriage through a period of drastic change is emotional interdependence between the spouses.

The Association lists among the most common marital crises illness, transfer to another city, the husband's unemployment, the need to take care of an aged parent and military service that separates husband and wife. The death of a child places a particularly severe strain on parents: a recent study of 40 couples with children who had leukemia found that 28 developed serious marital difficulties, and nine of the marriages ended in divorce soon after the death of the child.

Yet when the marriage is a sound one, it enables modern couples to weather crises, perhaps more readily than their forebears. The relationship between husband and wife is closer than any other in human society, and the shared strength flowing from this intimacy is a bulwark against bad times.

Women have always been expected to help their husbands cope, whatever the problem. But now husbands are helping their wives through a uniquely female ordeal. At right, Jim Hammer of Danbury, Connecticut, after staying at his wife Joan's side during the natural-birth delivery of their first child, gives her a kiss of joy and congratulation.

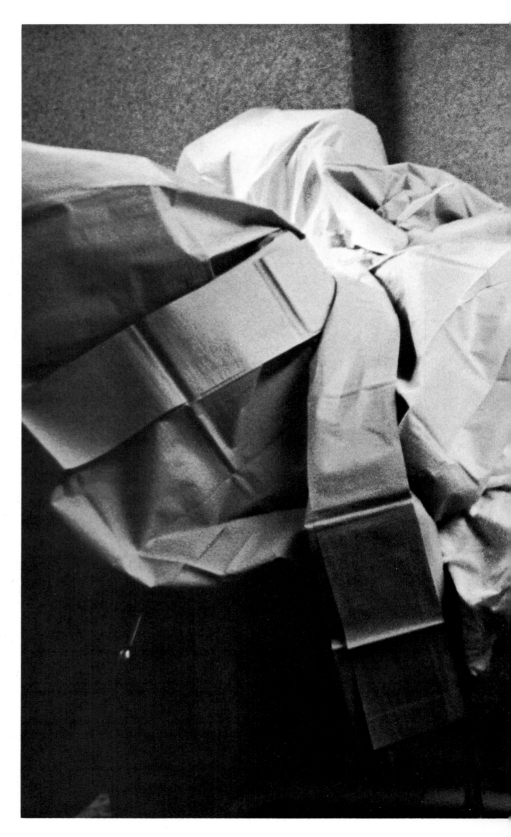

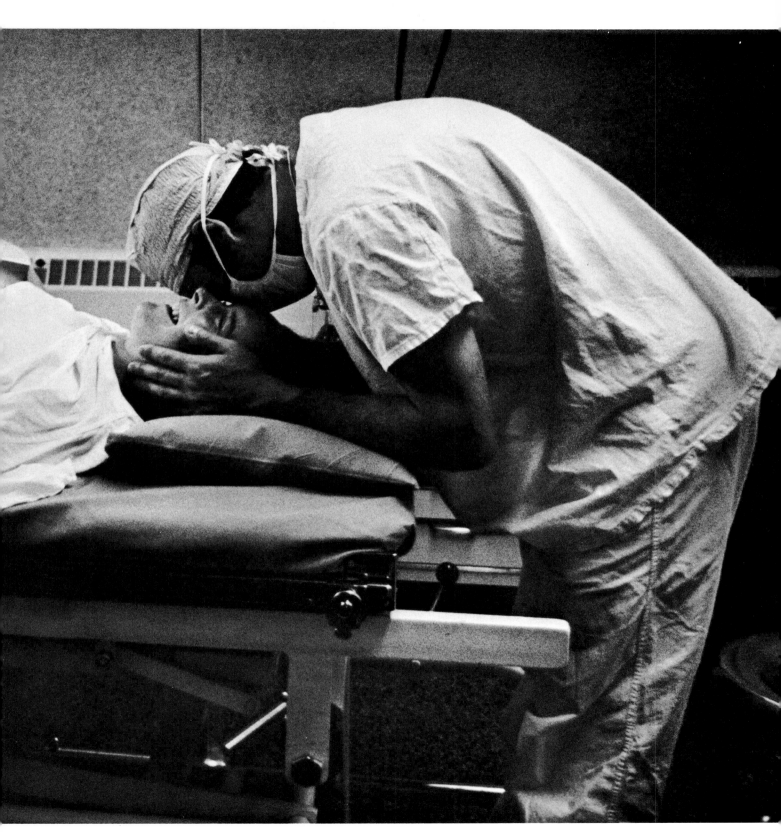

Parisian Jean-David Lefèbvre irons his wife Marie's slip as part of their down-the-middle division of housework. Marie and Jean-David, who have one child, both work in advertising—he as a production assistant, she as a stylist.

A better balance of labor and love

In 1973 a male schoolteacher in New York City, citing his desire to stay home and help his wife in the weeks after their baby was born, won his right to a paternity leave. Such leaves, already a government-paid option in Sweden, are a sign of a new division of labor between the sexes. Ever since the family was invented—perhaps a million years ago—women had stayed home to care for children while men provided protection and material support. Today an increasing number of couples participate equally in all aspects of homemaking. Fathers in New Haven, Connecticut, even work regular shifts at a cooperative day care center.

The other side of the new division of labor places some responsibility for family support on wives; often they are expected to be co-breadwinners with their husbands. In the United States, some 20 million out of 50 million wives work. And in Sweden, a woman who does not hold a job is termed a "luxury housewife" in government documents.

According to Warren Farrell, spokesman for a men's liberation group in the U.S., joint job holding improves the husband's lot by reducing his compulsion to get ahead. "When the woman is bringing in income," he says, "the man has a chance to experiment, and fail. He can try different work for a year or two, and if he loses the job, it doesn't put the family in the poorhouse."

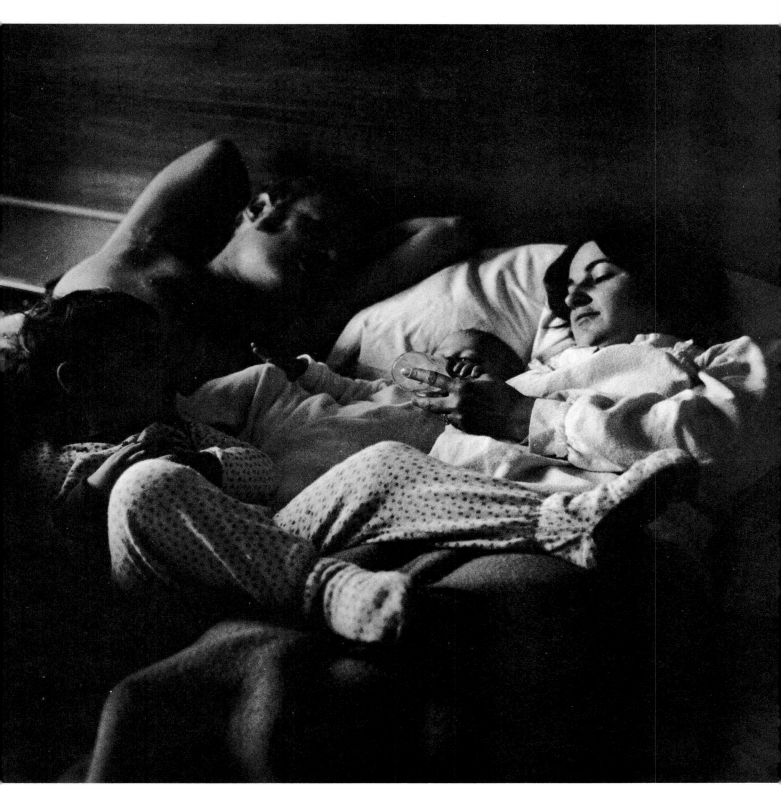

Paternal concern and maternal tenderness are balanced as the Palmer Beasleys of Seattle share a quiet moment with their two children.

Companionship: the lasting bond

In the old patriarchal marriages, companionship was seldom a consideration. Most wives were ignorant of the ways of men, husbands generally ignorant of women—and both thought it was meant to be that way. Both spouses went their own ways, finding friendship and sociability within their own sex. Not until women won the right to be educated and to join the work force were men and women generally able to meet and enjoy each other as persons.

Today, companionship is the hallmark of the successful marriage. In a study of American wives, 48 per cent ranked companionship as the most valuable aspect of marriage, ahead even of love, understanding, standard of living —or the chance to have children, which came in a poor second, with only 27 per cent of the vote.

Companionable activities mean not only husband-and-wife membership in the same organized groups—neighborhood associations, golf clubs, church guilds—but also simply an informative companionship, in which each partner makes a habit of telling the other things that happened while they were apart.

That companionship will continue to be the major objective in marriage is indicated by recent studies. One survey of 65 engaged men and women found that the choice of a marriage partner was made on the basis of compatibility and ease of mutual communication. Love was important, but it was not the romantic variety. Rather it was defined as a relationship that put the stress on the couple's ability to live together in psychological harmony.

Chatting comfortably at a 1954 coming-out party in Highgate, a residential section of London, a couple exchange impressions with the relaxed good humor characteristic of the deep, enduring companionship that men and women now expect of dating and marriage.

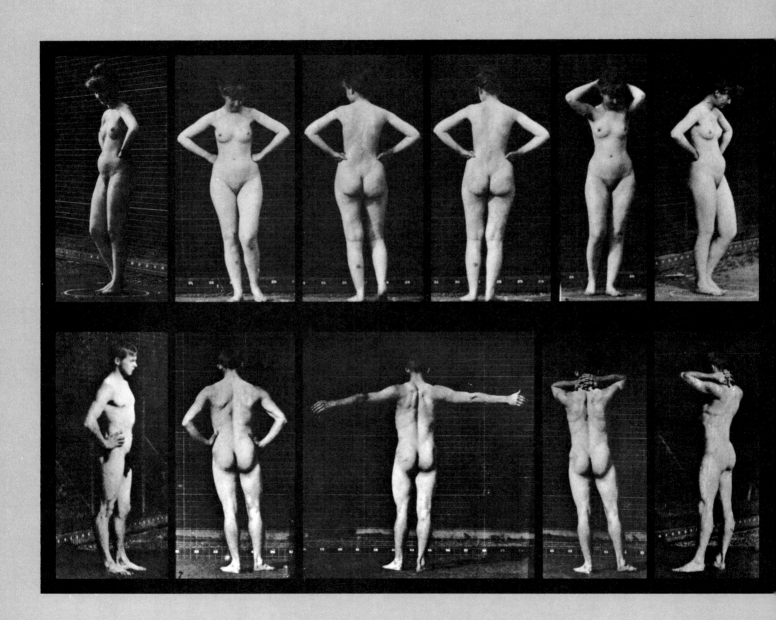

Physical Differences

2

"Anatomy is destiny," Freud once wrote. He was saying that biology shapes behavior; that men and women are destined by their dissimilar bodies to develop different needs and abilities, and to play distinctive parts in life. Freud was wrong. It is now clear that much of masculine and feminine behavior is learned, and it can be unlearned *(Chapter 3)*. But Freud was also right. Unalterable distinctions between male and female anatomies—some obvious and some only recently detected —establish that innate biology has a crucial bearing on behavior. These sex-linked differences seem to lie in three major areas: physique, emotions and mental ability. Men are generally bigger and stronger than women and they can run faster and throw harder. Men are more likely to fight someone than mother him. And while no one can say that men are smarter than women (or vice-versa), it has been clearly documented that each sex does possess aptitudes that are peculiarly its own.

Many sex-linked behavior patterns are as obvious as the anatomical differences so distinctly photographed *(left)* at the turn of the century by Eadweard Muybridge. Everybody's grandmother knew, for example, that boys are bigger and more physically aggressive than girls. What is new is that so few differences depend entirely on biology; learning matters more than anyone had realized. And grandmother could never have guessed the behavioral implications of biological facts. She did not know that although boys are stronger than girls, they are also weaker. Nor could she have imagined the ways biology establishes behavior for each sex. How babies are made is more a mystery than anyone had realized. Only now are scientists beginning to understand the interactions that convert a mother's egg and a father's sperm into a boy or girl and determine how that new being will act.

Differentiation of males and females begins at conception. It depends on a pair of chromosomes, the structures within cells that carry genes —minute biochemical blueprints. Each human cell contains 23 such chromosome pairs, one of each pair from the mother and one from the fa-

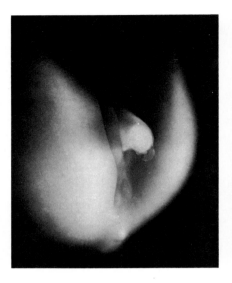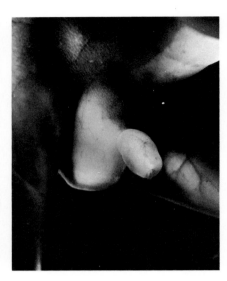

Growing out of the same bud, male and female sex organs look confusingly similar in their early stages—at right is the clitoris of an unborn girl three months after conception, at far right the penis of a boy in the fourth month.

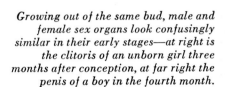

ther. But the sex of the embryo is fixed by one particular pair. There are two kinds of these sex chromosomes: one, rodlike, is called an X; the other, shorter and lighter, a Y.

At conception the mother's egg invariably contributes an X; that is the only kind of sex chromosome a woman carries. The father's sperm may contribute either a Y or another X. Coming together, the parental sex chromosomes form either an XX pattern, calling for a girl, or an XY combination, calling for a boy. At this point, the very beginning of a new life, the influence of sex is felt. For the odds favor the boy, or XY combination. The reason is simple: since the male, or Y, chromosome is lighter than the female X, as the sperm swim up the vaginal canal, those bearing a Y chromosome go a little faster than those that have to lug an X, and so they are slightly more likely to reach the egg first. The result is hardly inconsequential. More boys than girls are born: for every hundred female births there are about 104 male ones.

But while the smaller and lighter Y chromosome is responsible for bringing more males into the world, it apparently does little to make things easier for them once they arrive. More male babies die in childbirth than female ones, and more boys die in every succeeding year of life. By age 20, the number of surviving men and women is about equal; by 30, women are clearly ahead; and by age 65 there are only seven males for every 10 women. The life expectancy for women is greater than for men in virtually every country where it has been measured.

Apparently the Y chromosome weakens the male. How it does so is known in precise detail—but only with respect to a few of the many male failings. Certain physical defects are transmitted by the sex chromosomes themselves, which carry genes determining many of the characteristics that are passed along from one generation to the next. Each parent contributes one chromosome and the genes on that chromosome. The genes on X chromosomes always win the day. Thus if genes for a particular characteristic exist on both X and Y chromosomes in a boy, the X-borne gene overwhelms the Y-borne one.

This superiority of X chromosomes produces notable effects when the Y meets one of the 120 defects carried on the X. Color blindness is one of the simpler examples. The predisposition toward this weakness is carried on an X chromosome. In the female, this defect has a good chance of being countermanded by the matching gene on the other X chromosome. But in the male, there is no healthy X-linked gene to negate the orders of the bad gene; the weaker Y is no match for the powerful, defective X, and the baby will be born color blind.

Because males have no second X gene to protect them, color blindness and other X-linked defects and diseases—some types of congenital blindness, mental retardation and muscular dystrophy—are more common in men than women. But the best-known disorder of the X chromosome is hemophilia, a blood condition that slows the rate of clotting and makes even a minor fall a dangerous injury. The most famous chromosome that carried it belonged to Queen Victoria. The Queen herself did not have the illness, but one of her sons did. Her daughters and granddaughters went unscathed, but six of her great-grandsons were hemophiliacs, including Alexis, the last heir to the throne of Russia.

These royal case histories are a classic demonstration of the male genetic weakness. None of the queens or princesses developed the illness because she would do so only if the defective gene had been present on both of her X chromosomes; only one of the paired Xs carried it, and the bad gene was overpowered by the healthy gene on her other X. To acquire the disease she would have had to inherit it from both parents. For the unhappy princes, however, a single gene for hemophilia was sufficient, residing, as it does, on the male's only X. Since few hemophiliacs live long enough to reproduce and even if they do are unlikely to marry a carrier of hemophilia, the condition is rare among women.

Besides the X-linked defects to which men are especially vulnerable, some authorities think there are four conditions, passed on through genes in the Y chromosome, to which women are entirely immune. All of these defects are unfortunate though not lethal or even disabling: barklike skin, exceptionally hairy ears, thickenings similar to calluses on the hands and feet, and webbing between the second and third toes.

The list of diseases that can be linked specifically to genetic sex is fairly short. However, there are many other important diseases whose

Stutterers—all males—in a class at a speech school in England clench their fists and shout in unison in a confidence-building exercise.

The mystery of male stuttering

Stuttering is a universal speech disorder found in all ages and almost all cultures: the First Century Roman writer Vergil stuttered, as did the 17th Century English King Charles I and the 19th Century scientist Charles Darwin. It is no accident that these individuals were men—the ratio of male to female stutterers is 3 or 4 to 1.

Both upbringing and innate defects of male physiology have been blamed for the boys' impediment. Proponents of the environmental explanation point out that boys are usually expected to be more outspoken than girls and that if they are repeatedly forced to speak when they would prefer to remain silent, there is a possibility that they will develop hesitant patterns of speech.

Those who think stuttering is inherited connect the tendency to the fundamental maleness established by the Y chromosome *(page 40)*—not that there is any known connection to a specific gene but simply on the grounds that stuttering is another evidence of the masculine weakness that causes boys to have higher rates of infant mortality, birth injury and childhood diseases. It is possible that the muscle and nerve system that controls speech is less stable in a boy than in a girl, and therefore is more easily disrupted. Yet most experts agree that any organic cause of stuttering is reinforced by environmental pressures.

origins are unclear, yet whose sex orientation is obvious, and they make it plain that the weaker sex is male. There are only a few sicknesses to which women are more susceptible than men, chiefly diabetes and cancer of the reproductive organs. By contrast, there is a long list of physical afflictions that are more likely to strike men than women. To cite a few at random, men are more vulnerable than women to bronchial asthma and brucellosis, gastric ulcer and gout, harelip and hepatitis, tuberculosis and tularemia. They also suffer from heart disease more often than women, and they more often die of cancer. Some of these ailments seem to be inherited. Others may arise from possible sex differences in body chemistry or functioning that weaken the male's capacity to fight disease. Still others may single out males because of the jobs men choose.

Physical weaknesses are not the only characteristics, of course, that are ordained at conception when genetic sex is fixed. So, too, are the normal and obvious physical distinctions between the sexes. This differentiation begins to appear, however, only about six weeks after conception. It is at this point that the chromosomes shape the gonads, or sex glands, which can turn into either ovaries or testes. If the XX chromosomal combination orders the gonads to become ovaries, the gonads' outer rind does just that, while its core shrivels up. If the XY combination programs the gonads to change into testes, it is the core that develops and the rind that withers.

Even with the formation of ovaries or testes, the real work of producing a boy or girl is still to be done. What counts now is the presence, or absence, of certain substances, the male hormones called androgens —female hormones (estrogens) do not matter in this process. If the embryo is destined to become a male and has shaped its sex glands into testes, they begin to produce androgens. These hormones govern the development of the rest of the male sex organs. The internal sex parts grow out of two tiny ducts called the Mullerian and Wolffian structures (after their discoverers, German anatomists Johannes Muller and Kasper Wolff). Under the influence of androgens, the Wolffian ducts grow into the internal tubes that carry sperm, and the Mullerian structures wither away. In the absence of androgens, female sex organs develop: the Wolffian structures wither, while Mullerian ducts develop into the uterus, Fallopian tubes and the upper part of the vagina. In the same way the presence or absence of androgens shapes external sex organs. If androgens are present, a small protuberance becomes a penis, and a groove fuses over the scrotum. Without androgens the protuberance turns into a clitoris, the groove into the vulva.

The fact that these developments are influenced only by androgens

—only their presence or absence matters—has an obvious consequence: sex hormones are crucial to the embryonic male, and apparently only to the male. If something goes wrong before birth and an unborn baby boy does not secrete androgens or cannot respond to them normally, his male anatomy will never develop: despite his XY chromosome pattern, which ordered him to become a boy, he will be born looking like a girl. The embryonic female is not dependent on hormones for her sexual development. So long as androgens are absent, she will be born female. However, she will not grow up to be a fully developed woman unless her body receives estrogens at puberty.

The same thing is true of all mammals. Rabbits, for example, are always born female if the embryo's gonads are surgically removed before birth, regardless of whether their chromosome pattern is male or female. "The Book of Genesis had it wrong," says medical psychologist John Money of Johns Hopkins University. "In the beginning, God created Eve. You have to add something to get a male. Nature's first intention is to create a female."

The distinctions in reproductive anatomy preordained by biology are responsible for what Money calls the four "imperative" differences between the sexes: men impregnate, whereas women menstruate, gestate and lactate. Each of the four activities is performed exclusively by a single sex, the one that possesses the right anatomical equipment for it. These physical or anatomical functions are the most important distinctions between the sexes. They are characteristic of all normal men and women, and have a decisive bearing on the way they live their lives.

The other important physical differences, while more a matter of averages than absolutes, are also general consequences of biology. From the moment of birth and throughout their lives, males are generally larger, heavier and more muscular than females. When boys are born, they measure 20 1/2 inches on the average, half an inch longer than girls, and weigh seven and four fifths pounds to the girl's seven and two fifths. The man's respiratory capacity is greater because his lungs and trachea are larger. On the average, he takes about 16 breaths per minute, four to six less than most women, and his pulse rate is slower, about 72 beats a minute compared to 80 for women. He is generally taller (by an average of four inches in the Western world) and broader in the chest, with bigger hands and feet and more facial and body hair. His brows are likely to be heavier, chin squarer, and ears, nose and mouth larger.

Women are wide in the pelvis to accommodate an unborn child. Their feet and hands tend to be smaller and more delicate, with the fingers more often tapered. They have wider hips and heavier thighs, and they

A true-false quiz on the sexes

Some of the statements at right, all based on averages, are true, some false (an answer key is at the bottom). Many of these male-female distinctions arise from simple biological facts. For example, men's bigger, heavier bodies account for differences in the amounts of blood cells and water, and in the weights of brains, hearts, muscles and bones—though not of fat. The same cause explains differences in the energy needed to walk and in lung capacity and breathing rate.

Biology sometimes influences behavior directly: extra water in men's bodies affects the speed at which they get drunk, and women's wider hips and thighs influence their posture. It is less certain, but entirely possible, that innate biological endowments help determine such characteristics as aggressiveness, verbal and mathematical ability, and even life span.

Still other behavioral differences—in obedience and in concern over friends' opinions—seem acquired, not inborn. And one is as yet unexplained: a baby's readiness to smile depends on his sex, and no one knows why.

On the average:	true	false
1. Men's brains are heavier.	____	____
2. Men's hearts are heavier.	____	____
3. Men have more blood cells.	____	____
4. Women's bodies contain more water.	____	____
5. Men's bodies contain more fat.	____	____
6. Men breathe faster.	____	____
7. Women live longer.	____	____
8. Women use more energy to walk.	____	____
9. Men's muscles are heavier.	____	____
10. Men's bones are heavier.	____	____
11. Women are more inclined to be knock-kneed.	____	____
12. Women get drunk more quickly.	____	____
13. Girls are more likely to obey their parents.	____	____
14. Boys worry more about what their friends think.	____	____
15. Girls have less self-confidence.	____	____
16. Boys are more physically aggressive.	____	____
17. Girls are more sociable.	____	____
18. Boys are better at mathematics.	____	____
19. Girls have greater verbal ability.	____	____
20. Baby girls smile more than baby boys.	____	____

1 T; 2 T; 3 T; 4 F; 5 F; 6 F; 7 T; 8 F; 9 T; 10 F; 11 T; 12 T; 13 T; 14 T; 15 F; 16 T; 17 F; 18 T; 19 T; 20 T.

are plumper. Plutarch reports that when the ancients cremated the dead, they took advantage of this: "They whose business it is to burn bodies always add one woman to every ten men, for this aids to burn them, since the flesh of woman is so fat that it burns like a torch."

Some differences in the way men and women are constructed have familiar consequences in the world of sports. Most men outthrow and outrun women by a wide margin, and the reasons can generally be found in anatomy. When the arms are extended down at the sides with the palms forward, it becomes apparent that the man's upper and lower arm forms one even line, while the woman's forearm angles out from her body, presumably because her broad hip prevents it from hanging straight. This difference, along with a distinctive arrangement of bones in her shoulder girdle, makes it natural for a woman to throw with an underhand motion—she "throws like a girl," a distinct disadvantage in most kinds of ball games.

The bulging biceps, broad chests, muscular
legs and powerful hands of these turn-of-the-century
students in a wrestling class indicate the superior
physical strength that causes men to
be generally better athletes than are women.

Another crucial difference is in the way the pelvic bones are put together. To accommodate a fetus, the female abdomen must be larger than that of the male, and the ring formed by the pelvic bones must be large enough to allow passage of a baby at birth. As a result, the woman's pelvis averages two inches wider than that of the man, although the male pelvis—unlike most bones in his body—is both thicker and heavier. Moreover, the angle at which the pubic bones come together at the front of the pelvis is considerably wider in the female, averaging around 90 degrees as opposed to 70 degrees in the male. The fact that the woman's hips are wider and more prominent than those of the male has significant effects on behavior. She walks differently, swaying her hips, and her run is different—her heels kick slightly sideways rather than straight back, reducing the forward propulsive effort.

The results in athletics are predictable. A look at the record—almost any record—shows just how wide the margin of difference is, or rather used to be. In April 1911, Britain's *Strand Magazine* published a tabular and pictorial record of athletic performances and found that, on the average, men were half again as good as women. In some instances their superiority was even greater: they could vault twice as high and hit a baseball nearly twice as far. More recent comparisons tell an intriguingly different story when examined closely. World track records for 1974, for instance, are typical. In the javelin throw for men, Finland's Hannu Siitonen held top place with a record of 290 feet 7 inches, while the best woman, East Germany's Ruth Fuchs, managed 220 feet 6 inches. Dwight Stones of the United States made 7 feet 5 1/2 in the high jump against the 6 feet 4 3/4 inches scored by East Germany's Rosemarie Witschas. America's Robert Hayes held the men's world speed record for running, briefly achieving 27.89 miles an hour over a 100-yard distance, while the women's record, held by Wyomia Tyus of the U.S. stood at 23.78 miles an hour.

The surprising thing about these and other athletic performances is not that men beat the women, but the degree to which women are narrowing the margin. The gap was far narrower in 1974 than the half-again superiority of men in 1911. And in some events the best women have outdone the leading males. In the English Channel race of 1957, for example, the Danish swimmer Greta Anderson made it from France to England in 13 hours and 53 minutes, beating out 23 male and female competitors by more than two hours.

When the right kind of incentive comes along, women can perform some amazing physical feats. One instance: Florence Rogers of Tampa, Florida, lifted one end of a 3,600-pound car, 29 times her own weight of 123 pounds. Her incentive was powerful indeed: the car had fallen on her son when a jack gave way. (With less at stake, Josephine Blatt of the United States used a harness to lift a record 3,564 pounds—but that is far below the 6,270 pounds hefted by the male record holder, Paul Anderson, also of the U.S.)

There is a strange quirk in the comparison between male and female athletic abilities, however. Some of the women's feats have turned out to be questionable because a few astonishingly able women athletes have been exposed as frauds (males masquerading as females) or biological freaks (people whose sex is not entirely male but not normally female either). Some male athletes have also been accused of fraud for dosing themselves with male hormones to increase their strength and size.

One of the most impressive imposters was a German who became world high-jump champion under the name of Dora Ratjen in 1938 but

confessed in 1957 to being a man. (He claimed that the Nazis had made him masquerade as a woman "for the sake of the honor and glory of Germany," and added that he had found the life of a girl "most dull.") To uncover such deceptions, the International Amateur Athletic Federation in 1966 began requiring women athletes to be certified as female by a panel of doctors. Some of the athletes who were passed because their genital anatomy was female nevertheless looked remarkably masculine in many ways, so in 1967, the IAAF began demanding a more sophisticated sex test that can read a chromosome pattern in a few cells scraped from inside the cheek or a single hair pulled from the head. Since chromosome tests have become a must, several athletes have disappeared from the scene, presumably because they are not fully female. Most prominent are two Russians, Irina and Tamara Press, who hold many track and field records but were always referred to in locker rooms as the Press brothers.

Even with frauds discounted, the degree to which women have caught up to men in recent athletic competition seems to say something about the importance of anatomical differences. The men's superiority is innate—but it must be powerfully amplified by learning experiences. As women have been encouraged to take part in active sports, their proficiency has increased. At the time of the *Strand* survey, women had hardly attempted much more than a few decorous games of lawn tennis. Their performance since then, as their participation in athletics has expanded, has improved rapidly—more rapidly than men's.

Physical abilities like running and jumping are easy to measure; differences between the sexes become obvious and precise, and their connection to physiology can generally be traced with little difficulty. The second great category of sex differences—the emotions and the feelings that lie behind much visible behavior—is quite different. Judgments of distinctions are largely subjective, and causes are subtly complex. Yet there is often a biological basis for the fact that men act differently from women. It is now known that the cause, in many cases, lies with the sex hormones, androgens and estrogens. These chemicals may affect crucial aspects of behavior—mothering, aggression, depression, excitability. Even before birth, sex hormones apparently program parts of the brain so that some kinds of behavior come more naturally to one sex than to the other. There is some evidence from animal experiments that one example may be maternal activity. Both men and women can mother children, but women are quicker to act like mothers than men are. The phenomenon can actually be measured in laboratory animals. A mature female rat caged with newborn rats begins to mother

A modern symbol of the mythical earth mother, the ancient expression of the female's ability to reproduce, Cornelia van der Meij of the Netherlands holds her youngest in the proud company of her blacksmith husband and their 15 other children. Having borne a child each year of her married life, she was expecting her 17th when the photo was taken.

49

them instantly. In the same situation, a male rat initially ignores the babies, but after a few days he too begins to groom and cuddle them.

The close relationship between the sex hormones and emotions has been suggested by what happens when the hormone supply system malfunctions. From the animal studies and limited research on humans, it appears that if the hormones get switched—a boy is supplied with too much estrogen, a girl with androgen—behavior too may be transposed. The action of the hormones is a complex one, for the results depend on whether the error occurs before birth or both before and after.

The best evidence for this strange mixing up of sexes comes from experiments with rats. Females injected with androgen at a certain period before birth can become normal females, but if they get more androgen as adults, they then act like males: they attack true males and attempt an active male role in sexual activity with normal females. Males prenatally treated with estrogen sometimes develop normally until injected with more estrogen in adulthood. Then they lose interest in the opposite sex and behave like females trying to get the sexual attention of males. The experimenters theorize that injecting a rat with the wrong hormone programs the rat to respond to more of the same hormone after birth as if it were a member of the other sex.

The same kind of fetal programing occurs in dogs. When androgens are injected into female beagles both before and after birth, the dogs reverse a very familiar sex-specific animal behavior. Instead of squatting to urinate, these females make for a tree and lift one leg. In effect, parts of the brain have been masculinized.

There is one very suggestive—but still controversial—experiment indicating that hormonal confusion affects humans just as it does rats and dogs. Nature has performed inadvertent "experiments" in which prenatal mishaps have exposed infants to too much, or too little, of the hormones needed for normal development. Studying more than 230 such cases, John Money has concluded that in human beings as in animals, certain hormones may program the brain abnormally before birth and at least contribute to behavior after birth that is wrong for the individual's physical sex.

In one of Money's studies, he examined the behavior of 25 adrenogenital girls—that is, girls whose adrenal cortices had malfunctioned before birth, causing an excessive production of androgen. The girls, aged four to 16, were all genetic females—bearing XX chromosomes—but were born with male genitals, although not normal ones. All 25 were treated with plastic surgery and drugs so they would look female, and they were raised as girls. Money matched each with a normal girl

A sports champ among women

The mightiest female athlete of modern times was Mildred (Babe) Didrikson Zaharias. As a tomboy growing up in a small Texas town, she scorned dolls to work out on a homemade weight-lifting machine. She beat the boys at running and basketball, and earned the nickname "Babe" when she emulated Babe Ruth by hitting five home runs in a baseball game. At 18 she won gold medals in the 1932 Olympics for javelin throwing and the 80-meter hurdles.

In golf, the sport for which she became best known, she entered her first tournament in 1934; a year later, she won the Texas Women's Golf Championship, and in 1948 took the world championship. The Babe could outdrive most men golfers—she averaged 240 yards, compared to a male golfer's average of about 190 and a woman's of 160. Yet she recognized the physical superiority of the best male athletes. A few years before her death at age 42 in 1956, she said, "Talk about me having beaten male wrestlers, boxers and football players was the bunk. In fact, a girl wouldn't have strength to whop a really good male golfer."

In basketball, Babe made All-American.

She once pitched against the Dodgers.

Experts rated her a superb swimmer.

She was a hurdle champion in 1932.

Her Olympic javelin toss set a record.

In 1940 Babe took up a new game, tennis.

Golf was Babe's major sport for 22 years.

of the same age, race, IQ and background. Both groups of girls (and their mothers) were then interviewed and tested to discover whether their interests were traditionally male or female.

The adrenogenital girls turned out to be notably different, most dramatically in their preference for activities ordinarily preferred by boys. Twenty of the 25 were described as boyish by themselves, their mothers and their playmates. By contrast, very few of the normal girls took part in boys' activities and when they did it was for just a short while. The girls prenatally exposed to androgens enjoyed athletics; they preferred to play with boys and with cars, trucks and guns instead of dolls. Although the adrenogenital girls dressed up occasionally, they liked slacks, shorts and generally utilitarian clothing much more than frilly dresses. There is another kind of girl, of course, who likes to climb trees, plays roughhouse games, prefers the company of boys and bears a superficial resemblance to the adrenogenital girl. This is the tomboy

(pages 55-58) who actually is quite different from the girls in Money's experiments. The tomboy is a perfectly normal girl passing through a common phase. In contrast, the adrenogenital girl's masculine behavior is a long-term way of life, and she can be identified at birth by her abnormal genitalia.

The adrenogenital youngsters in the experiment often disliked babies. And while all of the normal girls with whom they were compared wanted children when they grew up and a majority said marriage was a very important goal, most of the adrenogenital girls either rejected the idea of having babies or looked forward to the prospect with a distinct lack of enthusiasm. To them, a career came first.

The few adolescents in the study followed the pattern of the younger girls. The adrenogenital teenagers were significantly slower than the normal girls to begin dating and less likely to have sexual fantasies. However, they showed no signs of lesbianism. "It appears that . . . the biological clock for falling in love was in arrears," Money reports, "but not that it was set to respond to a member of the same sex."

The 25 masculinized girls in this study were exposed to large amounts of androgen only before they were born. Afterward their hormonal balance returned to normal or was kept normal by drug treatment. Another, less fortunate, group studied by Money included 23 adult women who got heavy doses of androgen both before and after birth. The reason was that they grew up before 1950, when drugs to correct the hormonal error first became available. Most came into the world as hermaphrodites, and while all were brought up as women, the androgen secreted by their glands for years after they were born made them hairy, muscular, deep-voiced and generally mannish in appearance.

In most ways these virilized women proved to be very like the girls in the first study who looked but did not act feminine. Most had acted like boys throughout childhood, with little early interest in marriage or babies. But not unexpectedly, their sexuality was more often affected than that of the younger group whose hormonal balances were restored essentially to normal soon after they were born. Of the 23 in this group, 10 reported homosexual as well as heterosexual dreams and fantasies, and four had had bisexual experience. Still, not one felt she ought to have been reared as a man. More remarkably, 13 eventually married, although only two did so before drug treatment made them look and act more feminine. Despite misgivings about their ability to handle infants, five of the women had babies—indeed, one woman had three—and were successful in looking after them. Their success, plus the fact that some members of the group displayed little traditionally masculine behavior

In a tricycle traffic jam at a retirement village in California, only three of the elderly cyclists are men. The predominance of women reflects a key fact about the sexes: women outlive men, in the U.S., by nearly eight years.

53

even before the drug treatment began, indicates that even such powerful biological forces as hormones can sometimes be overcome by environmental influences. Research such as Money's has suggested the biological underpinnings for behavior that make an individual act generally masculine or generally feminine. The same basic cause—sex hormones—seems to have a direct influence on certain moods, such as depression, irritability and aggressiveness.

Aggressiveness has long been recognized as a male characteristic. There are dozens of careful studies to prove the observation holds true everywhere in the world. Under almost all conditions—in free play and in laboratory experiments, in France and Ethiopia, at one year or six —it is the boys who are more physically aggressive. One project involving youngsters from six different cultures showed that kindergarten and grade-school boys started more fights, made more threats, shouted more insults and were more likely to counterattack than girls from the same background. If aggressive demands are made on boys, they are likely to react aggressively, as if they enjoyed fighting for its own sake. When boys are shown drawings of violent behavior, they are more likely than girls to imitate it in later spontaneous play.

Interestingly, however, girls are fully aware of aggressiveness and use it in their own ways. When the girls in one study were offered a piece of candy for each of the aggressive actions they could recall from pictures, they remembered nearly as many as boys. But in real-life situations they relied on subtler pressures. One experiment in Los Angeles illustrates the kind of indirect aggression girls favor. Clinical psychologist Norma Feshbach organized 84 first-graders into two-child clubs, each with its special name and badge, and each with exclusively male or female membership. She then introduced a child from another class into each of the clubs and found that the boys were invariably nicer to the newcomer than the girls. "The initial response of girls to a new member, whether it be another boy or a girl," Feshbach reported, " was more likely to be one of exclusion and rejection."

That these distinctions in behavior, some obvious, some subtle, depend on sex hormones is not hard to deduce from millennia of experience with castration, the operation that cuts off the male body's main supply of male hormones by blocking or removing the source, the testicles. The ancients knew nothing of hormones, of course, but they had no doubt about the effects of castration. The fiercest of all so-called tame animals, the bull, was turned into the docile ox by castration. Men have also been castrated, accidentally or deliberately, with similar results. In West Germany, habitual sex offenders have been voluntarily

continued on page 59

Husky enough to compete on an even basis with the boys, Karla Cohn troops home after a swim with the gang—all male except for her.

The ways of the tomboy

Traditionally boys are supposed to play football and girls are supposed to dress their dolls. But many girls abandon conventional sex roles regularly enough to win half-derisive, half-admiring designation as tomboys—dynamos with the physical strength and temperamental assertiveness to win boys' acceptance. There are probably more of them than has been thought: in a 1974 study of U.S. college women, 78 per cent said they had been tomboys.

The origin of tomboy behavior is traced in one study to the stage when children, around age four or five, first become aware of the difference in size and strength between the sexes. Since the male is stronger, he appears more powerful in every way. His role is seen as more prestigious—and around age eight girls as well as boys may adopt it to improve their status.

Tomboys are apt to come from families that allow individualized development. Such was the case with Karla Cohn, the 10-year-old above, who was photographed by a family friend in 1955. The oldest of three children of a physician in a New York suburb, Karla was a tomboy for many years; yet she had a sister as girlish as Karla was boyish. The Cohns worried about Karla but did not pressure her. Eventually she changed, of her own accord *(page 58)*.

Karla cocks her right and leads with a
left jab at a friend of the family, while
brother Jonny cavorts underfoot.

Nimble-fingered but averse to needlework,
Karla uses her talent on a boy's project,
building a model ship. She will add it
to her collection of trains and planes.

Compelled to try on a new dress, Karla warily keeps jeans on underneath it.

Karla reaches down for a piece of lumber that Jonny boosts up to her during a repair job to strengthen the sagging floor of an old tree house the two share.

The only girl at a table of boys, Karla eats lunch in the school cafeteria. She had just two friends among the girls in her class. "All the others," she said, "like to play house, jump rope—that silly stuff."

Her tomboy days behind her, Karla at 14 is a shiny-eyed charmer flashing girlish smiles on a date with Robert "Tiger" Bethke—a boy with whom, only a few years earlier, she had played football.

castrated; they become docile (and more feminine in other ways).

Such general observations have now been buttressed by data from laboratory experiments on rhesus monkeys. When only a month old they display sex differences in aggression. The males wrestle, push, bite and tug; the females are shyer, turning their heads away when challenged to fight by males. In one experiment, androgens administered to pregnant rhesus monkeys produced newborn females that played more aggressively than normal females. Moreover, these prenatally masculinized females remained unusually aggressive as long as they lived. In another study, the dominant males of one rhesus group were found to have higher androgen levels in their blood than their more passive fellows. However, when the passive males were separated from the rest and caged with females they could dominate, their androgen levels rose.

If male hormones exert such a direct influence on a man's aggressive drives, female hormones would be expected to influence some of a woman's moods. Hormones, it is now known, are the cause of the swings in emotional feelings that in many women correspond to the monthly menstrual cycle. The outward effects of such emotional swings are dramatic: 49 per cent of female medical and surgical hospital admissions and most psychiatric hospital admissions of women occur on menstrual days and days that immediately precede menstruation. And although women are generally less violent than men, 62 per cent of violent crimes among women prisoners and nearly half of female suicides take place at those times. These peaks in emotional crises follow the extremes in the hormonal changes involved in the female reproductive cycle of ovulation and menstruation.

A 1966 experiment by two psychologists, Judith Bardwick and Melville Ivey, vividly demonstrated the link between mood and hormone levels. Bardwick and Ivey followed 26 normal college women over two cycles, testing them twice a month, once at ovulation, when hormone levels are high, and again just before menstruation, when they are low. The test required each subject to talk for five minutes about anything at all. Afterward the experimenters listened to recordings of the talks and scored them for self-esteem, hostility and anxiety.

Almost always, positive feelings were highest at ovulation, lowest just before menstruation. At ovulation, one typical subject reported, "So I was elected chairman. . . . I remember one particularly problematic meeting, and afterwards, L. said, 'You really handled the meeting well.' . . . It came out the sort of thing that really bolstered my confidence in myself." She told a different story premenstrually about learning to water-ski: "I was so clumsy it was embarrassing." In the same girl, anxiety was absent at ovulation. "We just went to Jamaica and it was fantastic." By contrast, her anxiety was high before menstruation: "I'll tell you about the death of my poor dog M. . . . Oh, another memorable event, my grandparents died in a plane crash. That was my first contact with death and it was very traumatic."

Acknowledging that this woman and the others in the study may have "anticipated their menstrual periods and were somehow responding as they thought appropriate," Bardwick then reports an unplanned control case that seems to negate this idea. Interviewed on the 14th day of her cycle when her hormone level should have been high and her mood confident, one young woman inexplicably showed great anxiety. The next day—two weeks before her expected period—she began to menstruate, indicating that at the time of her anxiety-filled interview, her estrogen level had actually been low.

Male aggression erupts into a slugging match between two boys. The sex difference in aggression appears around age two, and boys continue to be more ready to fight than girls through adolescence and college years.

In much the same way, a woman's mood may be even more drastically affected by the abrupt hormonal changes accompanying the menopause. These changes, which occur in the forties and fifties, are brought on by the decline of the hormone-producing function of the ovaries, and signal the end of the childbearing years. They are marked by waves of "hot flashes"—brief sensations of heat often accompanied by heavy sweating—and may be accompanied also by irritability, crying spells, confusion and hypochondria. The exact mechanism of these effects is not fully understood. One theory holds that the autonomic nervous system is dependent upon hormonal production for its balance and becomes disrupted when this production drops off. Another explanation maintains that the effects are more psychological than physical. The menopause is a landmark: a woman feels that with her childbearing years ended, she is growing old and life has lost its central purpose.

Girls express hostilities differently from boys. Like the child below bawling out a playmate on a Liverpool street, they usually express abuse verbally, perhaps because society condemns the use of physical violence on their part.

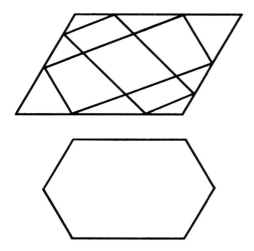

*Men score better than women in visual-
spatial tests like this one, readily
finding the simple form (bottom) that is
hidden in the complex pattern at top. (To
get it, drop the triangles at upper right
and lower left of the top figure.)*

Alterations in hormone production accompanying middle age also affect men's feelings, according to some authorities. Many men suffer emotionally during their middle years, exhibiting the tension and depression typical of menopausal women. While many experts think the cause is largely psychological, a few place the blame on the male sex hormone known as testosterone, which slowly decreases in quantity after about age 50. As long ago as the 1930s, internist August A. Werner of St. Louis University implicated hormonal imbalance in what has come to be called the male climacteric. He said, "With the exception of menstruation in the female, it is the same for the two sexes." More recently, the New York University authority on hormones, Herbert S. Kupperman, said, "There is no doubt in my mind—none—that these symptoms are due to the decline in testosterone production." While the interconnections between emotions and physical sex are painfully being traced as more is learned about hormones, the basis for a third major area of sex distinctions—mental proficiency—remains largely mysterious. As a matter of fact, it is only now that the magnitude and potential significance of these differences is becoming apparent. Although men's brains are a bit larger than women's, general intelligence seems to be equally divided between them; no test yet devised gives either sex an edge. But in certain special aptitudes one sex or the other is clearly favored by nature, and some of these peculiarly sex-linked aptitudes may illuminate larger areas of behavior.

On the average, girls surpass boys in the use of language. They speak earlier, learn to read sooner, are less often subject to speech and reading difficulties, and all through school score higher than boys in grammar, spelling and fluency. In mathematics boys are usually ahead from early adolescence on, beating the girls handily in analytic geometry, trigonometry and algebra. Boys study more mathematics and science than girls, and they do better at them even when less interested.

All of these facts suggest biological predispositions favoring one sex or the other. But environment makes an impact, too. When psychiatrist David Levy studied the family backgrounds of boys who were poor in mathematics but skilled at language, he judged the mothers to be overprotective. And psychologist Elizabeth Bing concluded from her research that girls who were better than most of their sex at mathematics had been handled by their mothers as sons are often treated: the mothers had always encouraged their daughters' independence and had frequently left them to study alone.

Differences between boys and girls have also been found in spatial reasoning and problem solving. Adolescent boys do better than girls at the flags test, in which a child looks at pictures of American flags and tells which ones have simply been rotated and which have been flipped over to create a mirror image. Boys also beat girls when shown a picture of gears and asked which wheel must turn to make some other part of the gear system move. In addition, boys are faster and more accurate at matching geometric shapes.

That the male's spatial superiority may be innate is suggested by comparisons between the spatial abilities of children and those of their parents. The high-scorers among boys and men are the children of high-scoring mothers, while the few daughters who do well are most often the offspring of spatially talented fathers. Scientists believe spatial ability may pass from mother to son and from father to daughter through a recessive gene that appears only on the X, or female, sex chromosome. That would explain both the prevalence of the skill in males and its occurrence in mothers and sons, fathers and daughters. If a son's single X

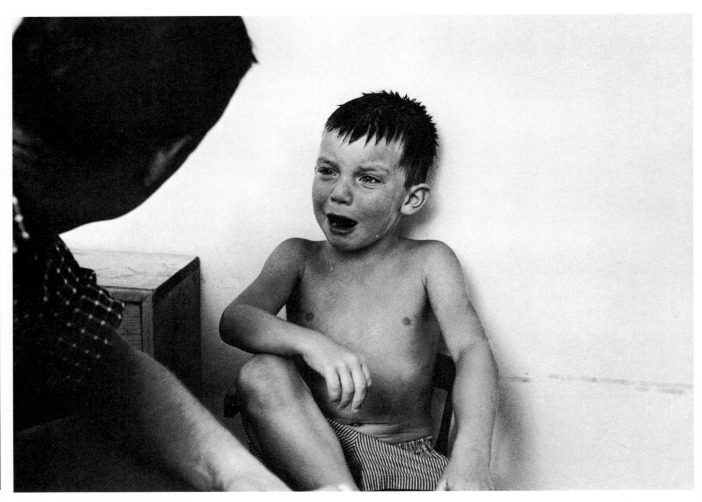

chromosome carried a spatial-ability gene, he would inevitably inherit the talent; a daughter would have two Xs, and since the talent-bearing one is recessive, she would inherit the talent only if it appeared on both.

Another special aptitude that may differ in males and females is a certain kind of analytical ability—the capacity to pay attention to visual details, to discard the irrelevant while abstracting single elements that will help to solve a particular spatial problem. People who possess this capacity are called field independent. Those without it are said to be field dependent. They tend to think globally, to respond to a situation as a whole. They cannot readily evaluate or even notice details because their perceptions are so much affected by the background, or field, in which the details occur.

The best known measure of field dependency is the "rod and frame test." The subject sits in a darkened room facing a luminous rod inside a slightly tilted luminous frame, and is asked to move the rod to a true vertical position. Using this test several investigators have found that males outperform females at many ages and in many cultures. Boys generally can separate the rod visually from the frame and make it stand upright. Girls frequently cannot ignore the frame; instead of adjusting the rod so that it stands straight, they place it parallel to the sides of the tilted frame. In a variant of this test, the subject sits in a tilted chair in a room that is also askew. Boys are generally aware of the tilt, but girls sometimes perceive both room and chair as straight even when they are off the vertical by as much as 63 degrees.

The interpretation of these results varies widely. Many authorities insist the field dependence of girls is learned, not inherited. And whether it is innate or cultural, it may be just a scientific curiosity with no influence on ordinary behavior. Some researchers, however, believe it is significant. They maintain that field dependent people are poor problem solvers because they are vulnerable to the influence of misleading clues. Field independence, on the other hand, is said to carry with it the ability to "break set"—to discard an old way of seeing and to find original and independent solutions to spatial problems.

The view of space may be linked to sex in other ways, according to psychoanalyst Erik Erikson. Erikson relates important mental attributes directly to anatomy and finds them expressions of the sex organs. He thinks that a small girl unconsciously senses the presence of the vagina and uterus, the "inner space" at the center of her body, and realizes its potential as the center of her procreative life. Her dim knowledge of her eventual fertility, he argues, makes her gravitate toward the receptive fulfillment of her inner self. Thus women are more likely than

Stopped from playing with a lawn sprinkler, a five-year-old boy bursts into peculiarly male tears of frustration: A study of three- to five-year-olds found that boys are more apt to cry than girls when they are frustrated—but girls cry more easily if they are hurt physically.

65

men to engage in passive contemplation of the inner mind. They are also more sensitive to the feelings of others and more ready to nurture them. Men are similarly affected by their anatomy, Erikson theorizes, and are consequently concerned with the penetration of external space, with technology, dominance, the manipulation of inorganic things and the management of worldly events.

Erikson supports his claims with evidence from a two-year study of 300 boys and girls between the ages of 10 and 12. He asked each youngster to arrange toys and blocks into "an exciting scene from an imaginary moving picture" and then to explain the plot of this film. Erikson's description of the results has been confirmed by other observers who studied a photograph of every child's construction without any knowledge of the child's sex or of Erikson's theory. The vast majority of boys built either high towers or houses that had "elaborate walls or façades with protrusions representing ornaments or cannons." People and animals were generally outside of buildings, and many automobiles moved along the streets, sometimes crashing in multicar pileups or else stopping on the command of a stern policeman. Girls tended to build peaceful interior scenes, with people and animals sitting or standing quietly inside low walls. Sometimes a girl constructed an elaborate doorway, and frequently her building was penetrated by animals or dangerous men. Of this feature Erikson wrote: "The idea of an intruding creature did not necessarily lead to the defensive erection of walls or the closing of doors. Rather the majority of these intrusions have an element of humor and of pleasurable excitement."

Erikson's provocative theory, like almost all others that attempt to isolate physical causes for the differences between men and women, is difficult to establish with clear-cut evidence, and many psychologists are skeptical of his findings. They question the assumption that small girls are even aware of their "inner space," and suggest that girls arrange toys and blocks one way while boys arrange them another, not because of sex-linked, innate differences, but because they learned from others to play this way.

Except for the all-important reproductive distinctions, it is never possible to maintain that all women are this way and all men that way. The other differences between the sexes are matters of degree, of tendencies and averages. Everywhere they overlap. Most men are indeed stronger than most women, but some men are weaker than some women. And while the best male tennis players are consistently better than the best women, the best women still can quite easily whip the majority of average players—male or female.

The Roles of the Sexes

3

In 1963 a young rural couple rejoiced in the birth of twin sons, both normal, healthy and attractive. Seven months later an accident destroyed the external sex organs of one of the infants. He appeared doomed to a tragic future. But his anguished parents decided to accept the counsel of physicians: "Bring the baby up as a girl."

The child was given a feminine name, hair style, clothing and toys. Plastic surgery began to reshape his physique, and hormone treatment was planned for later years so this transformed child could grow up to experience the sex life of a woman except for childbearing. Most important, the parents began to think of their baby as a girl and to treat her as one. Within a short time, she became noticeably different from her twin. When she was four and a half, her mother reported, "She doesn't like to be dirty. My son is quite different. I can't wash his face for anything. . . . She is very proud of herself when she puts on a new dress or I set her hair." The child born a boy had become a girl.

This remarkable reversal of nature illustrates the distinction scientists make between sex and gender. Sex means maleness or femaleness; it is a biological term that refers to the body. Gender means masculinity or femininity; it is a psychological term that describes thoughts, feelings and behavior. Gender has two aspects. One, gender identity, is the sum of an individual's feelings about his sexual status, his conviction that biologically he is either male or female. The other, gender role, describes a person's behavior, the part, masculine or feminine, that he plays in life. People are born either male or female, but they must learn to be masculine or feminine. The little boy and girl at left playing doctor and nurse in a South African school are learning gender roles deemed appropriate for their sexes. Conversely, the little twin boy was born male but learned to be feminine. Both examples dramatize the tremendous power of environment to determine gender roles.

This understanding of environment's potency is new. Until recently, it was assumed that biology decreed not only sex but also gender; that typically masculine ways of thinking and acting were laid down in the genes; that men and women, far from learning their characteristic roles, were born into them. The new importance attached to experience does not mean that biology has no part in gender development; learning does not take place in a biological vacuum. The inherited sex chromosomes, along with the male and female hormones, establish which sex organs will develop, internally and externally, and their appearance helps establish gender. Appearance signals adults to rear the infant as a boy or a girl and later influences the child, whose course toward masculinity or femininity depends partly on the way he himself perceives his body.

The single most important determinant of gender, experts believe, is the sex assignment that occurs at birth with the triumphant announcement, "It's a boy!" or "It's a girl!" This joyous affirmation sets in motion a whole chain of external events, ranging from the choice of a masculine or feminine name to distinctive child-rearing styles. These outward events, far more than the genes, determine whether the child will come to view himself as male or female and learn to behave accordingly. After all, a newborn infant knows nothing of anatomy, and therefore his first dim knowledge about his own sex comes from the behavior of other people. It is not long, however, before he begins to pay attention to his anatomy; indeed, the first few years of life are a time of remarkably uninhibited preoccupation with the body. A child also begins very early to notice the bodies of others. It is not known precisely how his perception of his own and others' sexual organs affects his gender development, but no one doubts that the effect is profound.

Late in his second year, an infant learns that human beings come in two distinctive types, and that he himself belongs to one or the other. This discovery has tremendous impact. In Sigmund Freud's view, it comes as a shock to a boy that the body of his mother, who is the center of his universe, is fundamentally different from his own. The realization comes slowly, usually after he glimpses the genitals of a sister or playmate. At first he imagines that he has in fact seen a body like his own. Then he assumes that the little girl has a small penis that will grow, but later, Freud says, he decides that she once had an organ like his but that it has been taken away as punishment. Terrified, he develops a castration complex, the fear that the same thing may happen to him.

His anxiety is intensified by a second important discovery, that his father is a powerful rival for his mother's affections. The growing son, thought Freud, harbors a secret wish to replace his father as his mother's sexual partner and is afraid that his father will sense his hidden desires and retaliate by castrating him. This rivalry Freud called the Oedipus complex, after the mythical Greek figure who slays his father and marries his mother. Freud believed that the complex marks the most dramatic crisis in the life of a boy, and that its resolution is the chief formative element in a man's personality. Eventually, the theory runs, the little boy gives up his infatuation with his mother both because he knows his wish for her will never be fulfilled and because he is frightened by his father's superior strength. His fear provides a powerful incentive to identify with his father instead of opposing him, and he resolves unconsciously to adopt the ways of men and to grow up as much like his father as possible. His attitude toward women remains permanently affected; he feels, Freud said, either "horror of the mutilated creature or triumphant contempt for her," imagining that "only unworthy female persons have thus sacrificed their genital organ."

The development of femininity in the little girl is different from that of masculinity in the little boy. Comparing her body with that of a brother or some other small boy, the girl reacts unequivocally to the discovery of his penis. "She has seen it and knows that she is without it and wants to have it," Freud wrote. Her intense jealousy, which Freud called penis envy, is accompanied by a resentful conviction that she has been maimed or at least cheated, and "she develops, like a scar, a sense of inferiority." Angry at her mother, whom she blames for her "deficiency," the little girl develops a feminine Oedipus complex: she turns to her father for love, hoping to get from him, and later, by extension, from other men, what Freud considered the psychological equivalent of a penis, a baby. Freud doubted that the girl's conflict could ever be as satisfactorily resolved as the boy's, and he was convinced that the girl's long-lasting penis envy doomed her to a kind of constitutional passivity, a hopeless quest to be made whole by someone else and an almost congenital dependence on the opinions of others. Many examples support his view. One mother reported that when her little girl watched a newborn brother being bathed the girl asked despairingly, "How can you love me when I'm so plain and he's so fancy?" Many psychoanalysts report that some adult women still consider themselves anatomically deficient, and that this sense of inferiority influences their behavior.

Freud's ideas about gender development have been criticized on several grounds. For one thing, a child can develop a clear gender identity long before he recognizes the anatomical differences between the sexes. Blind children almost wholly unfamiliar with these differences nevertheless know what sex they belong to and blind boys learn to identify themselves with their fathers, blind girls with their mothers.

Although critics of Freud contend that the theory of the Oedipus complex has not been scientifically proved, anthropologists have found few cultures that lack some signs of the Oedipal pattern, be it in myths, institutions or the experience of individuals. Interestingly enough, in societies where the biological father is not the dominant male in the family, sons rebel against whatever man plays that role. Among the Trobriand Islanders, the most powerful male in the family is the mother's brother—and sons have Oedipal dreams about their uncles.

The sharpest objections to Freud's formulation are aimed at his theory of female gender development and especially at his emphasis on the importance of penis envy. The psychoanalyst Erik Erikson, although essentially Freudian in outlook, has been one of the most articulate of those taking exception to the penis-envy theory. "It does not seem reasonable to assume," he wrote, "that observation and empathy, except in moments of acute or transitory disturbance, would so exclusively focus on what is *not* there." Erikson agrees with Freud that a girl's gender identity, like a boy's, is tied to anatomy. But he believes the girl is less affected by the absence of a penis than by the presence of the vagina and uterus, the anatomical "inner space," as he calls it, that will become the center of her procreative life.

No one knows, of course, if a girl can sense the presence of organs she knows nothing about. But at least one psychoanalyst, Robert Stoller, thinks she may be able to. He describes a girl born without vagina or uterus who became convinced that she could never become pregnant years before anyone informed her of her anatomical defect. "I told somebody I thought I was never going to have kids," she said to Stoller, "and yet I still did not know anything and I've never been able to explain that. I felt I couldn't have kids . . . and yet I don't know what gave me those feelings."

Stoller's patient became normally feminine despite her bodily deficiency—more evidence that anatomy plays a role, but only one role, in gender development. What a child feels about his sex depends less on what he was born with than on what he learns. Obviously this learning proceeds in many stages. First the baby must learn which sex he is. Then he must find out how his sex is supposed to behave in his society, from the reactions of others. In the earliest stages, when the child learns to identify his own sex, the process may be similar to one that in animal behavior is called imprinting.

Many birds and mammals develop certain adult behavior only if they undergo specific experiences at critical times while growing up. These experiences "imprint" themselves on the animal, shaping later activ-

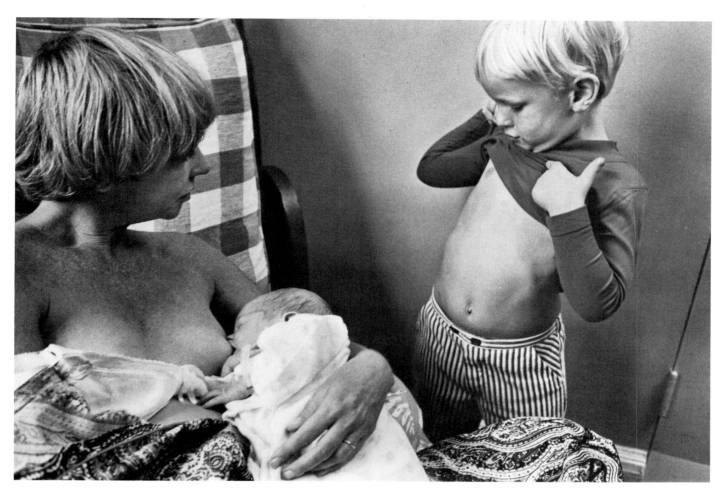

As his mother breast-feeds his sister, a bewildered four-year-old studies his own chest. For him, anatomical differences between the sexes are uncertain and confusing; when children of his age are asked to identify the sex of people in pictures, clothed men and women prove easier to tell apart than naked ones.

ities. A male mallard duck will be sexually attracted to a female mallard only if it associates with female ducks between 13 to 16 hours after it hatches. If a goose instead of a duck is present, then some system in the male will forever come alive at the sight of a goose. At maturity, it will be attracted by geese alone—and no later experience with ducks will change its preference. If only male ducks are around at the critical period, a male duckling will become homosexual.

A bird can even be sexually imprinted to humans, as ethologist Konrad Lorenz has demonstrated with greylag geese. At the time when they would ordinarily have become imprinted to their mother, he took her away and hung around the farmyard. The result can be seen in photographs showing the birds trailing the researcher. As goslings, the birds reacted to Lorenz as if he were their mother. As adult geese, their sexual urges were directed only toward him and other humans. Adult female geese, however attractive to normally imprinted males of the species, spurned the ganders and pined for Lorenz.

The process by which human infants learn their gender identity is not precisely parallel to the animal phenomenon of imprinting; untold baby boys have been brought up by men without becoming homosexual. Yet there is evidence that a baby is permanently bent toward masculinity or femininity in a critical period between 18 and 30 months of age. If he is treated either as a boy or as a girl during that interval, he adopts that gender; his so-called core gender identity, a conviction of belonging to one sex or the other, is fixed for life. The child himself is convinced of his sex at this early age. When psychologist Arnold Gesell, in his monumental study of child development at Yale, asked a group of three-year-olds, "Are you a little boy or a little girl?" he got the right answer from two thirds to three fourths of them.

Clinical evidence for the point of no return in the establishment of sexual identity comes from attempts to change gender. There have been many, undertaken for reasons less unusual than those that led to the transformation of the injured twin. It is not always easy to tell what sex a newborn baby really is, and some infants have sex organs that are neither clearly male nor unambiguously female. True sex can be established by chromosome or hormone analyses, but they may not be completed until months after birth—and then may show that the initial assignment was wrong. A child who appeared to be a boy may lack the Y chromosome of a male; genetically the child is female.

At Johns Hopkins University, where numerous cases of this kind have been studied and treated, experts may recommend reversal of the original incorrect assignment if the child is younger than a year and a half. They generally oppose reassignment later than that. For a child who has been treated like a boy for many months cannot be convinced that he is truly a girl—despite all attempts to do so.

Between the ages of three and six, children not only have decided which sex they belong to but also have learned something of the behavior expected of that sex. They quickly acquire a few stereotypes about gender role. Lawrence Kohlberg of Harvard University found that youngsters of four and five, male and female alike, thought men superior to women in physical strength, power and competence. He has also discovered that they understood violent behavior to be the province of men, and that they knew soldiers, firemen, robbers and policemen are likely to be male. In another study, done at Florida State University, Lydia Fauls and W. D. Smith noted a similar awareness of conventional gender roles among boys and girls of five. They showed each child a series of paired pictures of a child of his own sex. In one the child was doing something traditionally considered appropriate to

With somewhat heavy-handed gallantry, a Moscow auto worker waltzes his two-year-old daughter around the family living room as though she were a grown-up woman. Like most fathers, he encourages every sign of conventional feminine behavior on his daughter's part —and in return, by a process called complementation, she begins to master the arts of flirtation and coquetry.

his sex; in the other the activity was inappropriate. A boy, for example, was depicted first as playing baseball, then as playing with dolls. The experimenters asked each young subject, "Which do you like to do better?" Then they inquired, "Which does mother want the boy to do?" More often than not, a child replied that he preferred behavior commonly assigned his sex, and that his mother did, too.

Preferences like these are encouraged—and discouraged—by what the child sees others do. Children, like puppies and chimpanzees, imitate spontaneously for the sheer joy of it. A little girl copying her mother learns much that will stand her in good stead as she grows into womanhood. But her penchant for imitation may also lead her to acquire attitudes and habits inappropriate to a feminine role, at least as society sees it. After all, she observes both her mother and her father doing intriguing things, and she may take equal delight in copying both.

Each child, exposed to both masculine and feminine behavior, must learn to distinguish one from the other and then choose the right kind to copy. To do so, he must learn both gender roles, his own and that of the opposite sex. The child, in psychologist John Money's analogy, is like an actor who can play his part convincingly only if he knows the lines of the other characters in the play in addition to his own.

Easily distinguishable characters help the child learn his own part. He most easily understands both gender roles and best masters the one appropriate for him if his father is unmistakably masculine and his mother unambiguously feminine. They need not be masculine or feminine in traditional ways; a boy can become masculine even if his father does the laundry and his mother mows the lawn. Masculinity and femininity can be redefined if society so chooses, but they must remain definable, with at least some consistent and clear-cut differences between the parts played by fathers and mothers. "Children need roles to identify themselves with," psychoanalyst Martin Symonds says, "but you can't identify with a blur."

The dual nature of the imitation process is often characterized as identification and complementation. In the first, a child feels himself one with the parent of the same sex, and so he follows the behavior of that parent, not so much copying it consciously as absorbing it and reproducing it almost automatically; in a sense, he is the person his parent is. Complementation is the reverse. The child perceives himself to be unlike the opposite-sexed parent and instead of imitating him, behaves in an opposite fashion. A little girl treated in a courtly fashion by her father may respond with a coquettish glance like her mother's: this is both identification and complementation. A similar demonstration can be seen at any adult party attended by both sexes; the women act more feminine in the presence of men and men more masculine with women.

Important as they are, identification and complementation are not enough to explain how gender roles are learned. Boys without fathers to identify with usually develop typically masculine behavior anyway (though it may take them longer than boys from two-parent homes). Moreover, even boys who grow up in "normal" families with both parents may see their fathers very little, spending most of their days with their mothers or women teachers. As a result, psychologist David Lynn wrote in 1972, "The boy must learn from largely negative admonishments sometimes made by women and often without the benefit of a male model during most of his waking hours. . . . He must abstract the principles defining the masculine role." Unlike a girl, who can soak up femininity during long hours with her mother, the boy must figure out what masculinity means—often with not much more to go on than a barrage of don'ts ("Don't cry." "Don't touch your sister's dolls.").

Picking up a behavior pattern from repeated commands of "Do this" and "Don't do that" is the learning process called conditioning. Chil-

dren are rewarded for doing what is appropriate to their sex, be it making a dress or putting the shot, and they may be punished for attempting what is not. Most often the punishment is subtle rather than rough—and thereby, perhaps, all the more effective. When Mirra Komarovsky of Barnard College asked 73 college women to write out some of their memories of childhood, she was inundated with examples of the pressures exerted to make girls conform to stereotyped notions of femininity. "Mother got worried about my unladylike ways," one student wrote. "She removed my tops, marbles, football and skates and tried to replace these with dolls, tea sets and sewing games. When, despite her efforts, she caught me trying to climb a tree, she became thoroughly exasperated and called me a little freak."

The experience of another student demonstrated that pressure to be typically feminine continues into the college years. First she quoted from an exchange of letters between her and her brother. "What a wonderful evening at . . . fraternity house! I won all Ping-Pong games but one," she had written him. Then she quoted his reply: "For heaven's sake. When will you grow up? Don't you know that a boy likes to think he is better than a girl? Miss a few serves." His chiding stunned her, but she let herself be coerced—or conditioned. "To be a success one must date; to date one must not win too many Ping-Pong games," she told Komarovsky, adding, "At first I resented this bitterly. But now I am more or less used to it and live in hope of one day meeting a man who is my superior so that I may be my natural self."

Such examples of the influence of learning are often discounted. Skeptics point out that women who consistently win athletic contests with men are indeed exceptional, not because psychological pressures made them so but because biology did. There is other evidence, however, for the overwhelming influence of environment. Some of it comes from studies of diverse cultures in which masculine and feminine roles are seen to switch back and forth from society to society with no connection to biology. Perhaps even more persuasive is the new knowledge about sex reversals and sex confusions. It demonstrates that many males can be feminine and many females masculine; which gender they adopt depends on how they are treated.

Better than 99 times out of 100, sex and gender agree. Nearly always, a boy bears the XY-chromosome pattern in every cell of his body, secretes male hormones, possesses male genitals, knows he is male, and behaves in typically masculine ways. Nearly always, a girl carries the XX pattern. She is female not only in her chromosomes but in shape, features and psyche; she has no doubt that she belongs to the female sex,

Applauded by their fans, would-be beauty queens parade at Margate, England. Beauty contests vary enormously in importance and personnel—in Thailand the finals of the national contest dominate the news for a week, while in the U.S. five-year-olds vie to become Young Miss America. But wherever the competitions exist, they all glorify a socially acceptable ideal of feminine beauty and behavior.

and her ways are characteristically feminine. But there are exceptions. Once in a great while, an accident after birth, like the one that happened to the infant twin, makes it impossible to bring up a child in accordance with his genetic sex. More frequently, an individual's biological sex may be indeterminate because of some physical abnormality. Or his biology may be contradicted by his psychological feelings. A person with any of these problems can learn a gender that is independent of his sex.

Perhaps the most curious cases are people suffering from Turner's syndrome. They are born with cells having only one sex chromosome, an X. Possessing neither the Y of a male nor the second X of a female, they are sexually neutral. Externally, their bodies appear female, but they do not always have a uterus, they never have ovaries, and their bodies produce no sex hormones at all. At birth, their defects invisible, they are always presumed to be normal girls, and they are brought up as such. Despite their biological abnormalities, they develop a perfectly normal gender identity. They believe themselves to be female, and they act feminine. When Johns Hopkins University researchers compared Turner's-syndrome girls with normal girls of the same age, IQ and background, they found the two groups almost indistinguishable; both expressed similar interests in girls' toys and in romance, marriage and child rearing.

One Turner's-syndrome girl studied by Robert Stoller provides an especially vivid illustration of the way environment shapes feminine identity with almost no help from biology. Stoller's patient first consulted the medical center at the University of California at Los Angeles when she was 18 because her breasts had not developed and she had never menstruated. An exploratory operation revealed her lack of internal sexual organs. When she was told that she would always be sterile, her tearful reaction was exactly like that of a biologically normal woman. "I wonder what my kids would have looked like," she grieved. Although she was in most respects not biologically female, she dated often, liked to dance and to wear pretty clothes, and at school had always been most successful in homemaking courses. Her older sister described her as markedly feminine from childhood, telling Stoller: "She had a doll that she got when she was eight and she always said that she was going to save it to give to her little girl after she got married. . . . She was nine years old when my son was born, and she always loved to take care of him and was very, very good at handling him." The patient was treated with female hormones, and an operation corrected a vaginal deficiency. She later married, and Stoller has written,

continued on page 84

Having pitted himself against death in the ring and won, a victorious Spanish matador epitomizes the Mediterranean idea of machismo.

Arenas of masculine glory

The macho's arrogant stance is mimicked by a Puerto Rican boy in New York.

"Be a man!" That is the universal command to a boy. The process of learning to assert manliness begins early. Having been raised primarily by women, boys go outside the feminized atmosphere of the home to seek their own sexual identity. They do so by emulating their societies' more exaggerated types of masculine behavior: six-year-old Indians in Brazil test each other's toughness in mock duels; at the same age, youngsters in towns in the U.S. square off in imitation prize fights. As they grow up, men continue to congregate periodically in all-male groups where they exhibit to one another the prowess and skill of the he-man.

Certain forms of male display have recently come to be described as expressions of machismo (from *macho*, Spanish for male). Commonly associated in Latin America and many of the countries around the Mediterranean with the swaggering bravado of the bull ring *(above)*, machismo appears wherever males of any culture congregate in men-only surroundings: in English gentlemen's clubs, African tribal bachelors' huts, American fraternity houses and in Canadian male bars.

Displays of manliness range from barroom boasts about the conquests of women to arm-wrestling to initiation rites that test the endurance of applicants for membership in all-male societies. Whatever their nature, these events are almost always certain to be off limits to women.

Blending competitiveness and camaraderie, men the world over regularly get together to show off their masculinity. Above, Germans in a Munich tavern, bent on proving how much beer they can hold, raise high their steins while celebrating Oktoberfest, a 16-day festival during which they and their countrymen down approximately four million quarts of brew.

Two black men in Brooklyn greet each other in characteristic fashion: one extends a palm and the other hits it palm down. A break from the traditional handclasp, the gesture came into use as a mark of black male identity within the dominant white community.

The boys' night out in the United States often centers around a friendly poker game, testing male daring and coolness under pressure. Below, seven Florida men remain strong, silent and tight-lipped as the stakes grow higher and higher.

In Islamic societies, restrictions on women have made dancing mainly a male art. Above, an Arab shows his skill at an all-male wedding feast in Galilee.

"Her life as a female, as a woman and as a young wife is like that of innumerable biologically normal women."

Equally strong testimony to the power of the environment comes from the experience of males whose bodies do not respond to male hormones *(Chapter Two)*; they are born looking like girls, are raised accordingly and grow up feminine. A different kind of sexual confusion leads to similar results. John Money reports the cases of two hermaphrodites. Both had internal female organs, but the appearance of their external genitals was neither clearly male nor clearly female. One set of parents thought their baby was a boy and brought him up as one, while the other parents believed they had a girl and reared her accordingly. Both children were surgically and hormonally treated to make their appearance agree with the sex assigned them. As Money reported later, their "antithetical experiences signified to one that he was a boy and to the other that she was a girl." By preadolescence, the girl had a steady boyfriend and the boy a girlfriend. Of the boy Money said, "He fitted easily into the stereotype of male role in marriage"—even though "he and his partner would both have two X chromosomes."

Ordinarily, cases of discordance between sex and gender do not come to public attention. But the plight of transsexuals has now been widely reported because the facts are bizarre. These people suffer from no biological abnormality that present-day tests can detect. Yet transsexuals are firmly convinced from early childhood on that they are really members of the opposite sex. Biologically minded experts believe that a physical cause of this disorder will someday be discovered, and that it is likely to be a prenatal hormone disturbance. Psychologically oriented specialists, including Stoller, think that the cause is basically environmental. In several cases that he studied, the mothers of transsexuals seemed to want unconsciously to destroy their sons' masculinity. He concluded that they envied and disliked men and encouraged feminine behavior in their little boys. He discovered that because of their own psychological emptiness, some of these mothers held their male children against their nude bodies for so many hours and months on end that the children hardly knew where their mothers' bodies ended and their own bodies began.

Whatever the causes of the transsexuals' disorder, they want to change not only their life style but their sex organs as well. When George Jorgensen became Christine in 1952, sex-change operations were rare. By 1974 it was estimated that as many as 2,000 had been performed, the vast majority of them on men. Sex remains discordant with gender even in transsexuals who have had the operation; an operated male is still genetically male. "I don't change men into women," says Casablanca surgeon Georges Burou. "I transform male genitals into genitals that have a female aspect. All the rest is in the patient's mind."

Gender is in the mind, and male transsexuals can be convincingly feminine. One of the most famous cases, that of James Morris, demonstrates as much. Born in England in 1926, Morris seemed the epitome of masculinity. He served as a cavalry officer for five years, became a distinguished foreign correspondent, married and had four children. Yet as long as he could remember, he had felt himself to be a woman, and in 1972 he underwent a sex-change operation. "I feel myself at last," the new Jan Morris said. "I like being a woman. I like having my suitcase carried. I like gossiping with the lady upstairs. I like to be liked by men." Said an old friend, "In her blue tweed skirt and cream silk blouse, Jan looks like a cultivated, intelligent and handsome twin sister of the James she once was."

Cases such as these provide the clinical evidence that biology does

The coming of age of a young male is marked as a Jewish boy prepares to cut a cake at a party celebrating his Bar Mitzvah—his admission into the religious community. Traditionally reserved for boys, the ceremony is now, like many other such "rites of passage," less rigidly sex-segregated—in recent years a similar ritual for girls—the Bat Mitzvah—has become increasingly popular.

Skylarking girls of la belle époque

The ideal upper-class woman of the 19th Century was a placid soul. She could hardly be otherwise. Corseted in body, demure and submissive in spirit, most women led inactive, stuffy lives.

But not all women. As the century waned, some well-brought-up young ladies presaged the coming change in feminine roles as they shed their corsets in pursuit of a daring pastime —physical exercise. The bicycle gave these women a new freedom (one admirer described the bicycle as "the liberator of young womenkind"). Organized sports extended their social lives. And uninhibited pranks helped give them a new sense of themselves, almost a new identity.

No one documented the new spirit better than young Jacques Lartigue. The photographs shown here, now famous, record informal moments in the life of one well-to-do family and its friends during France's *belle époque* —the years from the 1890s to the outbreak of World War I—but in a deeper sense they celebrate the physical liberation of 19th Century women.

Supported by partner Charles Labouret, Lartigue's cousin Simone Roussel soars over the ice in a figure-skating contest. The two amateurs later won a world prize.

Skirt and petticoats flying, Simone applies the makeshift brakes of a homemade Lartigue contraption—a motorless gocart.

In a moment of pure high jinks, Simone cuts
an undignified caper in a forest glade.

Family friend Suzanne Lenglen, an international tennis champion in the making,
displays her form. Said Jacques, enraptured, "Her motions are music!"

not foreordain a particular role in life, that roles are learned, not transmitted in the genes. Another kind of evidence comes from anthropology. Much of what appears intrinsically masculine or feminine appears so only to the people of advanced industrial societies. In other societies, different patterns of behavior create quite different versions of masculinity and femininity.

Perhaps the most striking example of differences in views of gender comes from three New Guinea tribes that were studied by the doyenne of field anthropology, Margaret Mead, during the 1930s. Though the tribes lived within 100 miles of one another, subsisted on similar agricultural products, and shared similar languages and social traits, each had its own system of child rearing and marriage, and each also developed remarkably different notions of the ways in which men and women should behave.

The Arapesh, who occupied a difficult-to-cultivate range of hills inland from the Bismarck Sea, were a mild and cooperative people. Families were extended and informal, with warm friendships between even distant relatives, and much exchanging of long visits. Although men did most of the heavy labor, the sexes worked together in the yam and sago gardens that provided most food. Each Arapesh was expected to spend as much as half his time in the gardens of his relatives, and home building was likewise cooperative. Despite the poverty of the villages, gifts of food and chattels were frequently exchanged.

Marriages among the Arapesh were arranged; the bride was delivered to the home of the groom when she was seven or eight and he was about six years older. The husband consequently had a hand in the rearing of his wife. Both husband and wife were expected to share responsibility, and major decisions were made by the extended family. Birth ceremonies involved both husband and wife, and both partners were responsible for the welfare of the child. Children were breast-fed until three or four years of age, weaned gently, and as far as possible given whatever they wanted to eat. They were permitted a great deal of physical contact with their parents and other relatives and as soon as they could walk far enough, they were encouraged to follow their parents to the gardens, not necessarily to work, but more often merely to keep the parents company.

In such a society it is hardly surprising that the character traits most highly praised were those Western cultures view as feminine. This was true for Arapesh men as well as women. Aggression was frowned upon, and so strong was the pressure against overt hostility that a man who held a grudge against another usually assuaged his anger secretly—he journeyed down from the mountains and purchased a curse from the sorcerer of a lowlands tribe. Acceptance by peers appeared more valued than leadership, and self-respect was dependent not upon possessions or status but mainly upon the opinions of others. The Arapesh, both men and women, were sensitive and compassionate, quick to laugh, and rather passive and dependent.

If the Arapesh were, as a group, "feminine," the Mundugumors, who occupied a lush river plateau not 100 miles away, were "masculine." A warrior people who had practiced head-hunting until a few years before Margaret Mead arrived, the Mundugumors had not only captured rich farmlands where tobacco and coconut grew without much attention, but they had also driven other tribes out of a wide buffer area around their villages. Just as Arapesh families were organized to foster cooperation, so the social institutions of the Mundugumor seemed designed to set every man's hand against his brothers—and frequently his sisters and his father as well.

Mundugumor lineage passed down the mother's line, but relationships were also determined by a system known as a rope. A man's relatives, by this reckoning, included his daughters (but not his sons), his daughters' sons, and his daughters' sons' daughters. A man's behavior toward another's relative was fixed by these two systems into a complicated arrangement of guarded friendliness and outright hostility. Toward some kinsmen, he was expected to behave with respect and a certain amount of candor, while toward others an almost ritual bantering and exchange of insults was required. A child thus came of age in a rigidly prescribed hierarchy of personal relations, almost all of which were slightly hostile.

Child-rearing practices were similarly astringent. Children were carried about in rough-hewn baskets that could be conveniently hung on a rafter or tree branch when their mothers were occupied. They were weaned as soon as possible, and were thereafter roughly pushed from their mothers' breasts. Once they could walk, young Mundugumors were expected to fend for themselves—except that they were endlessly belabored to stay away from the fast-flowing river that ran through the heart of the Mundugumor territory. This reason, Mead believed, was not simply concern for their safety, but adult self-interest: if anyone drowned, the drinking of river water was taboo for several months, causing the whole community the hardship of treks to inland springs.

Perhaps the greatest hostility was reserved for relations between the sexes. Marriage was polygamous and based on a barter system. A man might receive a wife in exchange for one of his sisters or daughters. If too few sisters were available in a family, then brothers squabbled among themselves and with their father for the right to trade the young women. An older wife was in a dangerous position, anxious to keep her daughters for her sons' trading so that her husband did not barter them for younger wives. And if a man had no woman to exchange, he was forced to kidnap a wife from another village, or at least to induce an elopement—hostile action that almost invariably led to a counterattack by the offended villagers. Because the prestige of Mundugumor warriors was measured mainly by the number of wives and children they supported, the pressure to acquire wives caused frequent turmoil.

Mundugumor women were as strong-minded as the men and did not regard themselves as passive chattels. Adolescent love affairs, thought

to dishonor not the participants but their families, were often initiated by the women, and were frequently preceded by such violent foreplay that the lovers returned from the bush scratched and bloodied.

For all of the harshness of their upbringing, the aggressive Mundugumors were rarely moody or depressed. Even those at the bottom of the social ladder seemed good-humored, if not always satisfied with their lot. Indeed, the only Mundugumors who appeared out of place were those given to peacemaking and compassion.

Although the Mundugumor and the Arapesh seemed to be opposite in behavior, they shared one characteristic: compared with Western industrialized cultures, they were remarkably free of certain forms of sexual discrimination. It is not that women shared equally in political, or even domestic, power, but that they seemed to be motivated by the same drives as men. Among the Arapesh, both sexes were required to subordinate their individual wishes to the general needs of society; among the Mundugumor both sexes were expected to defend their rights with ferocity. In neither of the cultures was one sex expected to defer to the other. Moreover, the personalities of men and women were remarkably similar within each of the tribes. Mead wrote, "The Arapesh ideal is the mild, responsive man married to the mild, responsive woman; the Mundugumor ideal is the violent, aggressive man married to the violent, aggressive woman."

The third New Guinea culture that Mead explored, that of the Tchambuli, was different: in it she found sharp contrasts in personality between men and women. The Tchambuli were a small but highly skilled and comparatively wealthy tribe who lived on the shores of a fair-sized lake inland from the barren mountains of the Arapesh. Although they had once been warriors and takers of heads, they had become domesticated traders by the time Mead arrived. They found a plentiful food supply in the fish that they netted from the lake, and they also profited from commerce with their neighbors, bartering woven bags used as protection against mosquitoes. The families resided in solidly built dwellings referred to as the "women's houses," set high on the hills. Intricate dances and festivals were carried out in front of the men's gracefully carved ceremonial houses close to the lake shore.

The most conspicuous feature of Tchambuli society was the division of labor. Fishing and mosquito-net weaving were exclusively the work of women, who went unadorned, shaved their heads and were much given to loud and raucous humor as they hauled their nets by the lake. While men carried their wives' wares to market and often did the actual buying and selling, they took little part otherwise in providing for the

Under the eyes of a beaming teacher, Buddhist students prepare to assume the postures appropriate to religious discussion. As monks in a society ruled by religious leaders, these boys will help perpetuate Buddhist concepts of manliness—norms in their world but alien in the West. To them the ideal man shuns competition and material power, striving rather to be tender and compassionate.

community. The work of the men, who paid considerable attention to their dress and to their elaborate hairdos, was the creation of art: almost all of them were trained as musicians, dancers and wood carvers.

Polygamy was permitted but rare. Ostensibly, a man chose his own bride, paying a bride-price to her family, but in practice, courtship meant, for a man, a process of being chosen by a woman. In the early stages of child rearing, women regarded men as interfering nuisances. Boys and girls were treated alike until they were six or seven, when the women began including the girls in their work activities. The boys continued to spend their days in the harmonious atmosphere of the family dwellings until their initiation into adulthood, between the ages of 10 and 12; then they began their artistic training in the men's houses where they found a sharply different atmosphere. Generally ignored in the jealousies and petty conflicts that seemed to set the tone for adult men, the boys grew up devious, gossipy, passive, dependent on the opinions of others for their self-esteem, and, in many cases, neurotic. Girls, by contrast, became independent and well-satisfied women. "We found a genuine reversal of the sex-attitudes of our own culture," Mead summed up, "with the woman the dominant, impersonal, managing partner, the man the less responsible and the emotionally dependent person."

Weighing her findings about masculinity and femininity among Arapesh, Mundugumor and Tchambuli, Mead concluded that "human nature is almost unbelievably malleable," and that personality differences between the sexes are "cultural creations to which each generation is trained to conform." These findings (confirmed by many others), combined with the knowledge of sex reversals, convince almost everyone that environment far outweighs biology in causing behavioral differences between the sexes. Some people extend that view, suggesting that environment is not merely the principal influence on gender but also the only one; they maintain that all of the behavioral differences between the sexes could be wiped out. This radical belief seems to be wrong, for some activities seem always to be the province of men, others of women. Anthropologists are aware of no culture in which men take the primary responsibility for bringing up the young. In all known hunting and gathering cultures, moreover, it is the men who hunt swift and dangerous game, although women largely collect the vegetables and small animals that provide most of a community's food supply. And while the Tchambuli culture, along with that of several other societies, leaves the real control of affairs in the hands of women, there is no culture where political power is a female prerogative. Women may be sorcerers or healers, or the carriers of a written or verbal tradition, but in disputes arising outside of the household, known societies have generally given the tasks of adjudication, law-enforcement and punishment to men. Women are occasionally trained in the use of weapons, and female warriors are remembered by the Cheyenne Indians of the United States and a few other groups. Nevertheless, the Amazons were creatures of myth, and in no culture have women served as the principal warriors.

Such general behavior patterns, observed everywhere in all times, are what anthropologists call cultural universals. "In every culture of which we have any knowledge," Margaret Mead says, "public life and achievements outside the narrow realm of the family have been more the concern of males than of females, and the care of the home, the hearth, and the children has been more the concern of females than of males." Some behavior may be interchangeable, but in certain important respects the roles of the sexes remain separate and distinct throughout the world.

Pigeonholing men and women

"You might as well give her a gorgeous pen to keep her checkbook unbalanced with," advised an advertisement a few years ago. "A sleek and shining pen will make her feel prettier. Which is more important to any girl than solving mathematical mysteries." The advertisement was capitalizing on familiar stereotypes of the sexes—women are not supposed to be smart, only attractive.

Such pigeonholing of people is not confined to advertising. It is engaged in by films, books and television as well. Women are depicted as sex objects, scatterbrained and kitchenbound. Men are portrayed as decision makers, authority figures and conquering heroes. The stereotyping falls into two major categories. One projects an ideal: the woman or man who arouses envy or admiration by suggesting beauty or success. The other is a caricature, an oversimplification that amuses the observer and makes him feel comfortable because human behavior has been reduced to readily recognizable and predictable patterns.

Both kinds of stereotyping serve as handy labels for quick recognition, and they often are entertaining. However, they also reinforce rigid concepts of the sexes, pushing people into traditional patterns of behavior whether they are suitable or not. The woman who can keep her checkbook accurately balanced —with or without a "sleek and shining pen"—understandably resents the implication that she ought to pretend to be ignorant of mathematics, lest her ability detract from her feminine appeal.

The allure of pretty airline stewardesses was used in a provocative advertising campaign to attract air travelers, raising charges of sexism and exploitation that the airline steadfastly denied.

Selling with stereotypes

A tattooed arm makes beer a man's drink.

CARLING
Black Label
The lager to stay with...

STAYING POWER

Black Label

L'AIR DU TEMPS
Parfum de NINA RICCI

A dancer's grace is linked to perfume.

„Mein bestes Rezept für Püree heißt Pfanni, weil's so locker wird. Und wenn Sie mein bestes Rezept für Kasseler wissen möchten, schreiben Sie mir."

Pfanni
Püree

Ihr bestes Rezept für Püree heißt Pfanni. Weil es flocken-locker ist.

A pretty housewife promotes potato mix.

Mother love is the theme for Italian soap.

A heroic airman pushes British tobacco.

A Spanish businessman sells machinery.

Field & Stream takes you to A Man's Place

All your senses are alive to enjoy a day like this in A Man's Place. You're ready to appreciate the easy taste and great outdoor aroma of Field & Stream pipe tobacco.

A quality product of Philip Morris U.S.A.

An outdoorsman appeals to pipe smokers.

Type-casting on the screen

In an Indian movie the irresistible romantic hero ardently woos his swooning love.

Vivien Leigh is the idealized belle in Gone With the Wind, charming a male crowd.

The archetype of the sex kitten, Brigitte Bardot, plays her own cliché.

In the popular British film, Alfie, Michael Caine portrays the philandering male.

William Powell holds court as the autocratic patriarch in Life With Father.

Storybook heroes and heroines

The handsome prince peers at Snow White in a German edition of the tale.

Even in Pakistan, Hester of The Scarlet Letter is marked with A for adultery.

A conventional career for women is endorsed by an English children's book.

In an Italian story, a suitably fearless hero rescues his sweetheart from pirates.

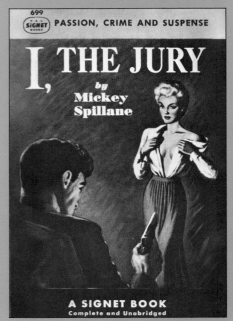

Disrobing at gunpoint, a Mickey Spillane heroine seems both virginal and seductive.

A stereotypically nagging wife berates
Rip Van Winkle for irresponsible ways.

Stalwart men fend off science-fiction
monsters in a French comic strip.

Stock images on television

The mother who knows best is played by Inge Meysel, center, on German television.

The swashbuckling adventurer is epitomized on Japanese TV by a samurai.

On American TV the fearless Daniel Boone leaves for a frontier exploit.

Lucille Ball sets a pattern for the scatterbrained housewife in I Love Lucy.

In an Italian soap opera, the improvident heroine is given money by her father.

The Sexual Revolution

"Sex isn't the best thing in the world, or the worst thing in the world, but there's nothing else quite like it," the comedian W. C. Fields said once. Few would dispute his conclusion that sex is unique. Yet on all other aspects of this most intimate and essential of male-female relationships, equally few would agree. Sexual activity has been vilified and praised, proscribed and encouraged, damned as sinful and glorified as holy. In a few societies (inevitably short-lived ones), it has been banned altogether. But in all cultures of record, it has always been regulated, more or less. Over the centuries, the regulations have swung back and forth in severity between the license of ancient Rome and the prudery of Victorian England, but perhaps never have they altered so abruptly and universally as in the 20th Century—the young people at left frolicking in the nude at a rock festival in Louisiana would have been thrown in jail for such behavior only a few years earlier. All over the world, traditional attitudes toward sex have been broadened—or abandoned—in a sexual revolution that is perhaps the most significant development in human behavior today.

Many causes for the revolution can be identified. Reaction against repressions of the past played a part. The drive for equality for women gave them sexual rights as well as political and economic ones. Advancing technology—factory work, urbanization, even the automobile—drastically altered family life. Contraceptives made sexual activity possible without increasing family size. The influence of religion weakened. Scientific study demolished old myths and began to give the world its first clear understanding of sex.

The forces behind the sexual revolution have been felt even in the most tradition-bound countries. A sex manual has been published in the U.S.S.R., a bastion of puritanism; women's view of sex is changing in Italy and Japan, where female submissiveness has been the rule. In America and to a somewhat lesser extent in Europe the code of acceptable conduct has been overturned. Masturbation, sex before and outside marriage, and even homosexuality are openly discussed and freely advocated. After hundreds of years of hand-wringing over the end of virginity as a "loss," the "ruination" brought by unchecked desire, and the "debasement" of public and private morals, it is fashionable to believe that the only danger in sexuality lies in curtailing it.

Sex has been transformed from a private secret to a subject for almost obsessive public debate. Topics that might have made a gynecologist blush in the 1950s are discussed on national television in the 1970s, and words like bisexual and orgasm, once the exclusive vocabulary of clinicians and researchers, appear on the covers of magazines displayed for every member of the family to read. These outward signs announce a profound change in the public view of sex: it is no longer a duty, distastefully accepted by women and guiltily enjoyed by men, but a natural activity to be undertaken in many forms by people of all ages for pleasure as well as procreation.

The idea that sex is a pleasure to be enjoyed freely by everyone is hardly a 20th Century invention. Pagan writers extolled sex. In 2 B.C., the Roman poet Ovid published the *Art of Love*, a work with a surprisingly modern ring. "The wise shall choose as it suits him; one and the same delight does not enrapture us all," Ovid said.

Not until the early Christian era were the joys of the body condemned as sinful. The one man most responsible for the change was the Carthaginian professor of rhetoric, born in 354 A.D., who became St. Augustine. As a young man, Augustine delighted in sex and wanted to grow up to be like his virile pagan father, Patricius. But Augustine's mother, a convert to Christianity named Monica, opposed his licentious habits. She entreated her son to abandon his mistress and give himself to religion. To escape his mother's pressures, he fled to Rome. But she tracked him down, insisted on moving in with him and continued to harangue him about his lusty way of life. Agonizing over his wish to turn to religion and please his mother and the conflicting desire to continue his intensely sexual life, Augustine prayed, "Give me chastity and continency, only not yet."

The American psychoanalyst Charles Kligerman believes that Augustine's struggle was not religious but Oedipal, a battle to save his masculinity from his mother's jealous assaults. According to Kligerman's Freudian interpretation, Monica wanted to keep her son away from other women; she unconsciously believed that if he joined the church, he would "belong to her forever." In the end, Monica got her way: Augustine renounced sex and was baptised a Christian. Then he began to set down on paper some of the harshest indictments of sexuality ever written. Procreation in marriage, he said, was the only excuse for sexual activity and engaging in it for any other purpose—even as an act of love—was sinful. His tirades against sex, along with those of later theologians, influenced the lives of people in the Western world in every generation to the present.

Most social historians agree that Christianity gave the Western world (and parts of the Orient) a distinctively troubled view of sex. Instead of being a natural pleasure to be enjoyed under certain limitations, sex became a shameful indulgence. On the one hand it was recognized as necessary to human survival, but on the other it was considered sinful. Abstinence was an ideal to be emulated. There is less agreement about why converts to the new religion so willingly took up an idea that called for so much self-denial. Apparently Romans were ready for a change. As pagan eroticism degenerated into excess it aroused a revulsion against unrestrained sex; forbearance, the giving up of luxuries and pleasures, seemed the proper response to a time when the civilized world was disintegrating into the Dark Ages.

Deeper explanations for the taint attached to sex have been sought by some authorities in primitive fears and fantasies, which linger in the most modern of human beings. Hugh Northcote, a moral theologian, suggested in 1916 that because a love-making couple is easy prey for attack, early man usually chose a secluded spot for intercourse; sex became private and hidden, and like many concealed activities aroused feelings of guilt. A somewhat different analysis was made in 1925 by sociologist Edward Westermarck of the University of London. The idea that sex was evil he ascribed to a kind of instinctive tendency to look on it as "defiling, or in other words, as a mysterious source of danger." In many cultures, Westermarck wrote, a woman is thought of as basically unclean: "Particularly during menstruation, or when with child, or at childbirth, she is supposed to be charged with mysterious baneful energy—no doubt on account of the marvellous nature of these processes and especially the appearance of blood." Later Westermarck commented, "It is strange to think that such crude notions have for ages exercised a dominant influence upon the moral attitude towards sex behavior in Western civilization. While the original notions have vanished, they have left behind feelings and views which, however irrational, have survived more or less even to the present day."

Such explanations for the sinfulness of sex, however, may raise more questions than they answer: If guilt is so instinctive, why is the instinct seldom expressed outside the West?

A gallery of controversial art

At the unveiling of Michelangelo's Last Judgment in 1541, an impressed Pope Paul III sank to his knees in prayer. In 1558, however, Pope Paul IV had draperies painted over "provoking" parts of the figures—and during the puritan Counter Reformation painted skirts and breeches were added to the draperies.

In one social setting or another, each of the works on these pages has outraged its viewers. Each has also been accepted by some people as fine art.

Paintings and sculptures of nude human bodies have a way of arousing such responses. Through these works, artists evoke the physical roots of eroticism and sensuality. At the same time they must, if they can, remain within the boundaries of the permissible. The double task is all but impossible: sooner or later, a work of art in which the nude body is incorporated will run afoul of local taboos.

As the examples illustrate, the ways in which an artwork can become offensive to society are as diverse as art and society themselves. A painting may be accepted in one period and rejected in another; a statue may be simultaneously welcomed and spurned in two different cultures; in the same culture, at a given moment, a work may be forbidden at one level of opinion and adopted with great enthusiasm at another. Most puzzling of all, an artist such as Manet, with deep roots in the accepted traditions, may produce an image, like the one shown on the opposite page, that his audience finds problematic and disquieting.

But all of these responses have one point in common: they reveal more about the attitudes of a particular society toward sex than they tell about the works of art that become the focus of those attitudes.

When Auguste Rodin's The Kiss was exhibited in Paris in 1898, one critic exclaimed: "A masterpiece!" But in prudish America, during the same decade, the entwined lovers were deemed unfit for public exhibition at a World's Fair, and the work was relegated to a private room with admission by application only.

Officialdom delivered a clear judgment on Paul Chabas' September Morn, painted in 1912. "Too little morn and too much maid!" snorted one authority, while another pronounced the painting "definitely illegal." But the public took the insipid picture to its heart, buying seven million reproductions as well as "September Morn" novelties that ranged from umbrella handles to sailors' tattoos.

For his Luncheon on the Grass, Edouard Manet borrowed the device of a nude woman among clothed men from a painting by Giorgione—a work accepted without a raised eyebrow. Yet Manet's version shocked viewers, perhaps because he painted a very real 19th Century woman—a "commonplace woman," said one critic, who "shamelessly lolls between two dandies dressed to the teeth."

In Christian society, the extreme sanctions urged by Augustine were quickly modified—abstinence strictly observed by all the faithful would surely lead to extinction (as it has among certain celibate sects, such as the Shakers). Over the centuries the trend has been one of continuing liberalization—but not without wide swings in attitude. Under the first Christian emperors, molten lead was poured down the throats of men who helped prostitutes find clients; persons not united in wedlock were forbidden to kiss each other. In Calvinist Scotland in 1605, people known to have engaged in sexual activity without benefit of clergy were fined and put in irons. The town of Perth employed a man whose duty was to shave the heads of "fornicators and fornicatrixes," and other towns ducked, pilloried or expelled offenders. By the time Charles II of England was restored to the throne in 1660, his subjects were beginning to react extravagantly against the strictness of the Puritan regime that had exiled him. Charles himself took an endless succession of mistresses. He did not trouble to conceal them—at least 13 are known by name—and he had no qualms about publicly recognizing 14 illegitimate children as his own. To engage in open adultery during his reign was a way of demonstrating loyalty to the crown, and wildly uninhibited behavior became common among the highborn.

By Victorian times, the pendulum had swung to the opposite extreme, and people embraced the notion of sex as sin. Explains historian Crane Brinton, "Recurring phases of . . . Puritanism in sex matters are in Western history usually symptoms of deep-seated social problems—as are recurring phases of widespread sexual license." During the reign of Victoria, from 1837 to 1901, the problems were those of an age of transition. The growth of industry had disrupted old life styles, while the rise of science had cast doubt on long-cherished beliefs. Middle-class Victorians sought refuge in domestic tranquillity. Women were exalted—not as women but as mothers, pure, ethereal beings whose function, according to a popular guide for wives written by Sara Ellis, was to lift their husbands' minds to a "higher state of existence." Their sexual interests were supposed to be nonexistent. Physician William Acton expressed the typically Victorian opinion. Normally modest married women, he wrote, "are not very much troubled with sexual feelings of any kind," because "love of home, children and domestic duties are the only passions they feel."

The prudery of the times turned the suggestive word "legs" into "limbs" and required that they be covered even when they belonged to furniture. Such priggishness seems now, when nude couples can be watched making love in movies and on the stage, to belong to the distant past, yet it persisted until World War I. Its end was preordained by the very forces that brought it about. For if the complex of social change initiated by the Industrial Revolution at first stimulated Puritanism, it also stimulated scientific inquiry into human behavior. These investigations eventually turned to sex. What the studies revealed prepared the groundwork for the sexual revolution of today.

Among the scientists who began to study sexual conduct were anthropologists—it was always more or less acceptable to describe the sexual practices of peoples considered primitive. Perhaps the most important contribution of the anthropologists was their discovery that sexual mores are almost as various as cultures are numerous: a code of conduct that one people accepts as a mandate from on high often strikes another people as shockingly immoral. Reading about the exotic sex lives of alien peoples was titillating to Western readers, but it had more serious effects as well. Confronted with wide varieties of sexual behavior, and with primitive man's openness about sex and his sometimes frank enjoyment of it, the Westerner was compelled to reconsider his own values.

Anthropologist George Murdock estimated that no more than 5 per cent of the societies he knew about placed an absolute ban on sex before marriage. Another 20 per cent or so considered it wrong only for women, not so much on moral grounds as to guard against illegitimate births. This left 70 per cent that allowed premarital intercourse under at least some circumstances.

Many tribes in Indonesia, New Caledonia and South Australia permitted even very young children to engage in sexual activity. In 1897, Sir Harry Hamilton Johnston claimed that among certain Central African states "there is scarcely any girl who remains a virgin after about five years of age." And Herman Heinrich Ploss reported that the Valave of Madagascar permitted—in fact, encouraged—youngsters, occasionally brothers and sisters, to have intercourse while adults looked on. Societies in which sexual relationships were postponed nevertheless paid a great deal of attention to small children's genitals. Among the Balinese, wrote Margaret Mead, "A little boy's penis is being continually teased, pulled, flipped, flicked, by his mother, his childnurse, and those around him. With the slight titillation go the repeated words, 'Handsome, handsome, handsome,' an adjective applied only to males. The little girl's vulva is patted gently, with the accompanying feminine adjective, 'Pretty, pretty, pretty.' "

Although studies of remote tribes taught Westerners something about

The irrepressible profession

The exchange of sex for money is one of the oldest and most durable of human transactions. But the status of the principal figure in this transaction, the prostitute, is constantly changing. When the status of women is low, the prostitute's will be relatively high; in ancient Athens, where many wives were little more than illiterate slaves used for procreation, husbands bought sexual favors of hetaerae, courtesans of education and social grace.

When wives are valued for their sexless delicacy, prostitution will be seen as hygenic sexual release; at the end of the 19th Century, many countries in Europe licensed brothels and medically certified prostitutes. In the U.S. police tolerated and even supervised the operations of red-light districts.

In most Western nations today, at a time of rapidly changing customs, the role of prostitution is changing too. In the U.S., for example, with sexual freedom on the increase, fewer men are initiated to sex by prostitutes, and fewer men have premarital intercourse with prostitutes. But efforts—like the one below—to stamp out prostitution usually have little lasting effect.

A madam (face covered) and one of her prostitutes are escorted from a bordello in Los Angeles during the course of a police raid.

their own sexuality, sex research in the West itself did much more to liberate men and women from old inhibitions. This work vindicated sex. It has been pursued in recent decades most vigorously in the United States, notably by Alfred Kinsey and William Masters and Virginia Johnson. But the pioneers in the field were Europeans, products of the Victorian age: the physicians Havelock Ellis and Sigmund Freud.

Ellis devoted most of his life to a compendium of sexual behavior, *Studies in the Psychology of Sex*, published from 1896 to 1928. A true son of his time, Ellis had sexual difficulties of his own. He did not have intercourse until he was 32, and until he was 59 he could not enjoy sex with women he cared about. Nevertheless, he believed in the then radical notion that sex is natural and desirable. "The person who feels that the sexual impulse is bad, or even low and vulgar, is an absurdity in the universe, an anomaly," Ellis wrote. "He is like those persons in our insane asylums who feel that the instinct of nutrition is evil and so proceed to starve themselves." Ellis shunned any narrow definition of what is normal and was tolerant of the abnormal, maintaining that if adults "privately consent to practice some perverted mode of sexual relationship, the law cannot be called upon to interfere."

Freud's contribution to the cause of sexual liberation is even greater, if only because his work is better known. Freud believed in sex for pleasure as well as for procreation. Although he by no means advocated casual sex, Freud said he could not support conventional morality because it "demands more sacrifices than it is worth."

The pioneering efforts of Ellis and Freud helped make sex research respectable, and the first organization for the scholarly study of sex was established in 1911 in Berlin. But systematic sex research has always been chiefly an American phenomenon. Between 1915 and 1947, Americans published 19 sex surveys based on questionnaires or interviews. Although a few of these investigations were sound, many others are suspect because the approach was prudish. Many questions were so delicately phrased that it must have been impossible to know what the researcher wanted; sometimes the investigator's Victorian bias encouraged replies that were less than candid. In 1926, one state health officer asked his subjects, "Has anyone ever tried to give you the mistaken idea that sex intercourse is necessary for the health of the young man?"

It was not until the late 1930s that straightforward and nonjudgmental inquiries were conducted. At that point Alfred Kinsey and his colleagues at Indiana University began to interview some 17,000 men and women to secure material for two monumental reports, the 1948 *Sexual Behavior in the Human Male* and the 1953 *Sexual Behavior in the Human Female.* "Evasive terms," Kinsey once said, "invite dishonest answers."

It is a surprising fact that Kinsey himself, at least at one stage of his life, was not without sexual inhibitions. According to Wardell Pomeroy, one of his chief associates in sex research, Kinsey once told about a college friend who had confided that he masturbated and was profoundly worried about it. Shocked, young Kinsey proposed that he and his friend kneel down at once and pray that the friend be granted enough self-control to end this "sinful" practice.

Kinsey spent most of his youth and early middle age in fields far removed from the study of sex. He earned his doctorate in entomology from Harvard in 1920, eventually became a professor of biology at Indiana, and over a period of 20 years collected not sexual histories but about four million gall wasps. He traveled 80,000 miles to find them, often taking his wife and children along as assistants. Mrs. Kinsey has told how she encountered a snake on one field trip and called out to her husband for help. "Just kill it," he shouted back, letting his wife fend for herself while he went on with his search for insects. His transition from an obscure expert on gall wasps to the world's foremost authority on sex came about almost by accident. Kinsey was widely respected on the Indiana campus for his personal probity and known for his conservatism. These traits led to his selection in 1937 to teach a new course in sex and marriage. A trip to the library convinced him that more was then known about the sex habits of wasps than of American undergraduates, and he began to apply to human sexual behavior the professional biologist's techniques of observation and analysis, using recently developed statistical methods. At first he interviewed students and university employees, asking them explicit questions about their erotic lives; he had collected 733 histories by the end of 1939. Over the next decade, his extracurricular interviewing developed into a full-time occupation and led to the founding of the Institute for Sex Research.

Kinsey and three other investigators traveled the United States for 15 years, collecting information in prisons, saloons, burlesque theaters, offices and private homes. They recorded their data in code to protect the privacy of their informants. Kinsey was adept at finding subjects. In New York's Times Square, he would walk into homosexual bars and announce, "I'm Dr. Kinsey, from Indiana University, and I'm making a survey of sex behavior. Can I buy you a drink?" In Naples, he would choose a rainy night to talk to prostitutes and madams so there would be fewer customers to interrupt. He was a gifted interviewer. The actress Cornelia Otis Skinner, one of many well-known people who told

Havelock Ellis pioneered the scientific study of a then-taboo subject with the publication in 1897 of the first of his seven-volume Studies in the Psychology of Sex. Advocating objectivity and tolerance for sexual activity, he urged that researchers "get at the facts, and . . . look them simply and squarely in the face."

him their most intimate secrets, said later, "He has the skill of a great actor in drawing you into what he is doing. He attracts you like a magnet. You forget all your fears and have complete confidence in him."

When the Kinsey reports were published, they created a furor. What should have seemed the least surprising finding was taken as the most dramatic: Americans, it turned out, were hypocritical. When it came to sex, they ignored traditional moral precepts and the law itself, rarely practicing what they preached. From a reading of the Kinsey findings along with the prohibitions laid down in the nation's statute books, it appeared that most Americans were unconvicted felons, and that presumably pathological or morally corrupt behavior was statistically normal or at least remarkably popular. Some 92 per cent of the men in Kinsey's sample, along with 62 per cent of the women, said they had masturbated at some time in their lives. More than 80 per cent of the married men interviewed were sexually experienced before marriage, and so were nearly half of the women. By the time they were 40, half of the husbands and 26 per cent of the wives had had an extramarital affair. Nearly half of all the people in the study had participated in some variety of oral sex, an activity widely considered perverse (and today still illegal in most of the United States). As for homosexuality, about half of the men admitted to at least one experience with it, as did 28 per cent of the women.

Kinsey's interviews with "normal" men and women confirmed what Freud had learned from his neurotic patients: that erotic life begins much earlier than many people choose to recognize. Some parents reported that they had observed children three years and younger masturbating; in one case, the child was four months old. Significant numbers of men and women said they had begun engaging in sexual activity or had experienced sexual feelings by the time they were five, and nearly an eighth of the women and close to 40 per cent of the men had taken part in sex play between the ages of five and 12.

What Kinsey did not confirm was the then prevailing view of women and sex. Few women were frigid. True, men did have more orgasms than women. But 25 per cent of the female subjects had experienced orgasm by the time they were 15; 50 per cent by age 20; 75 per cent by age 25 and 90 per cent by the age of 35.

Another important discovery was that sexual behavior varies widely; few people fit any statistical average. In general, religion and social class were found to be important influences. Orthodoxy was more important than any particular religion. Catholic, Jewish and Protestant women in their twenties were about equally likely to have had sexual ex-

Their gazes swiveling after a young woman who seems dressed for the occasion, a group of young Italians in Rome's Piazza di Spagna enjoy a round of girl-watching. The practice is universal but frowned on almost everywhere except in Italy. There, public ogling of women and appreciative comments on their appearance form an acceptable channel for sexual impulses and fantasies.

117

perience outside of marriage, but within each of the three religions, devout believers were less than half as likely to engage in such activity as those whose religious participation had lapsed. Class differences were marked among males, but not among females. College men were much more apt to masturbate frequently and almost three times more likely to pet to the point of orgasm than their noncollege contemporaries, but they typically began to have intercourse later in life. At the age of 20, half the college men in the study were still virgins, while among those who did not attend college, the figure was only 20 per cent. Kinsey had seen hints of this class difference when he began studying sex at Indiana. In later years, he sometimes spoke of a campus policeman who believed students abnormal because they spent so much time lying under the trees in each other's arms. As Kinsey said, "Sexual intercourse the policeman could understand; but this interminable petting must be some form of perversion!"

Although Kinsey's work was initially questioned on the grounds that the people he talked to were not representative of the public, these charges were not entirely warranted; his sample was properly selected to give an accurate reflection of white Americans—the basic group of broad interest. Later studies have largely confirmed the Kinsey statistics. A more direct approach to sex research—observation of actual sexual activity—had been taken by a few investigators in France, Germany, Japan and the United States, who watched sexual activity and published observations. Kinsey himself made direct observations at Indiana in the 1940s, reporting his findings—without saying how he had arrived at them—in his 1953 report in a chapter called "Physiology of Sexual Response and Orgasm."

But no one had conducted precisely controlled laboratory studies of human sex on a large scale until William Masters, a gynecologist, and Virginia Johnson, a one-time music student with a flair for psychology, began their program at the University of St. Louis in 1954. Masters and Johnson started by observing a group of 11 prostitutes, but they soon found that many ordinary people were willing and able to perform under the eyes of the researchers. Eventually the two observed 694 men and women, among them 276 married couples, ranging in age from 18 to 89, photographing their reactions and measuring their heartbeats, brain waves and body temperatures. For the first time the physical effects of sex were objectively recorded. The heart rates more than doubled in some cases, and blood pressure nearly doubled.

Human Sexual Response, the book that reported these data, was published in 1966. A dry physiology text, it nevertheless sold 300,000 copies by 1975. Its chief conclusion was that under laboratory conditions, at least, an orgasm is an orgasm, a physiological happening that progresses through four phases, which the researchers labeled excitement, plateau, orgasm and resolution. The stages are the same in both men and women, and the measurable physical effects are the same no matter how the orgasm is induced.

The Masters and Johnson research directly challenged some traditional and firmly held beliefs. The finding that orgasms achieved by any means are alike physiologically (if not necessarily psychologically) was welcomed by some militant feminists, who felt it freed women of dependence on men for sexual satisfaction. A somewhat related observation indicated that penis size does not directly affect response. But perhaps most significant was the laboratory evidence that backed up Kinsey's data: sex is not just for the young, or just for men. It is enjoyed by males and females of all ages.

Both men and women can be sexually active in their eighties, the investigators found. "All that is needed," Masters says, "is reasonably good health and an interested and interesting partner." And the idea that sexual pleasure is largely a male prerogative was shattered by the records: The women Masters and Johnson observed were at least potentially capable of five or six orgasms in quick succession, each one, in many cases, more intense than the last; some subjects, artificially stimulated, had from 20 to 50 orgasms in the space of an hour.

The St. Louis investigators did more than measure sexual behavior. They also developed a new way of helping sexually unhappy people. Most psychiatrists believe that the major sexual difficulties in Western society are caused by deep emotional conflicts and can be cured only by resolving those conflicts in psychotherapy. Masters and Johnson think that a simpler approach will often set things right sexually, and that once this is done, a couple may be better able, with or without psychiatric help, to face underlying problems. They maintain that sexual performance, like tennis or swimming, can be learned and improved with practice. More important is their belief that sex is "the ultimate communication," that enjoyable sex is impossible unless both partners want to give pleasure, and that sexual failure takes two people: one partner alone is never to blame.

These ideas are put into practice in the treatment of sexually troubled couples at the Reproductive Biology Research Foundation in St. Louis. In the office of the stern-looking Masters and the more outgoing Virginia Johnson, a husband and wife begin by giving their sexual histories. Then, over the next 10 days or two weeks, they are directed to go to the apartment provided for them and, in privacy, caress each other gently, perhaps stroking the back or tracing the outline of arm or thigh. The idea is to give—and receive—pleasure without feeling any pressure to perform sexually. Every day they report their progress and are given further instructions; occasionally they may be told not to touch at all but just to enjoy each other's company at dinner and the theater. Eventually they move on to sexual caresses and at last to intercourse, learning special techniques to help with particular problems.

Between 1959 and 1975, Masters and Johnson tried to help 1,827 men and women, with varying degrees of success. They were able to help about three fourths of the men troubled by impotence, and 98 per cent of the men affected by premature ejaculation. When they worked with frigid women, their success rate was 81 per cent. Keeping track of patients by telephone, they found that of those who had responded favorably in St. Louis, 95 per cent were still doing well after five years.

Sometimes the results of treatment seemed spectacular. One couple came to Masters and Johnson when the husband was 61 and his wife 58. In her whole life, she had never had an orgasm. Yet on the surface, at least, there was little to explain their sexual failure. Both came from warm families. Although their parents had avoided talking about sex, both husband and wife had been sufficiently uninhibited to experiment sexually before marriage. Married 28 years, they enjoyed sex even though they were disappointed because the wife had missed an important life experience. They were resigned, however—until, according to Masters and Johnson, they noticed "the mutual excitation and physical attraction between their son and his fiancée." Then they decided to seek treatment; their problem was solved in 10 days.

Such success stories only strengthen the major criticism of the St. Louis researcher-therapists' work. To many people, their approach to both investigation and treatment dehumanizes sex. New York psychoanalyst Natalie Shainess charged that their mechanistic outlook robbed sex of its joy and meaning. Existential psychoanalyst Rollo May suggested that Masters and Johnson were fighting puritanism with "the new technology," a dangerous weapon, he said, because it depersonalized sex by assuming that sexual activity was part of technology. Yet an understanding of the mechanics of sex is essential to a rational philosophical and moral view, and this understanding is Masters' and Johnson's great achievement.

It is impossible to prove that sex researchers' findings are responsible for what has been called the new morality; one of the curious phe-

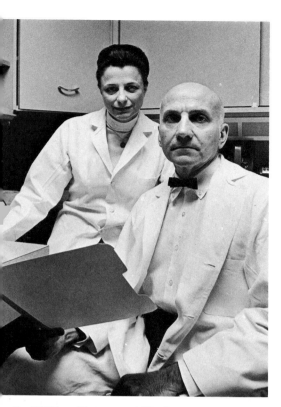

Dr. William Masters and Virginia Johnson (above), whom he later married, reported the first large-scale direct observations of human sexual behavior under controlled laboratory conditions. Outside the lab they turned to therapy, with a program of counseling and training to remedy sexual inadequacy.

Alfred Kinsey was first to provide a firm statistical base for the study of human sexual activity. His case histories of American men and women, compiled from 17,000 interviews and published in 1948 and 1953, revealed an extraordinary range of sexual behavior, varying widely with education and social class.

nomena of social history is the regularity with which new ethical ideas seem to call forth scientific evidence that supports them. It does not really matter whether the egg or the chicken came first. It is a fact that a sexual revolution has been going on for a long time throughout the Western world, and, to a far lesser degree, even in the Orient.

If changes in scientific understanding have reduced the authority of large segments of the old sexual code, what remains is not exactly a moral vacuum. A new set of values has emerged, and though it is hardly universally accepted, nor in any way complete in its particulars, it has acquired a certain moral suasion of its own.

Its first, and basic, premise is that sex is healthy. Sexual difficulties, so the new argument runs, come not from the unrestricted indulgence of erotic desires but from denying sexuality and limiting sexual self-expression. Indeed, anything involving the body that feels good and does no harm to others should be accepted, while notions of modesty, cleanliness or fashion that keep people from enjoying their bodies should be discouraged. What is natural, so the theory goes, is beautiful.

The second major assumption is that sexual relationships should be based on equality. If sex is a form of self-expression then it follows that both sexes should be equally free to make demands in a relationship —and required equally to shoulder responsibilities. Sexual stereotypes should be abandoned, allowing room, for example, for the naturally passive and dependent parts of a man's character or the aggressive impulses of women. As a result, the "double standard," which encouraged sexual experimentation among men while prohibiting it among women, has essentially disappeared in many cultures.

Finally, those institutions such as marriage or child rearing that seek to regulate sexuality should be as flexible as possible. They should be able to reshape themselves around the idiosyncracies of individuals —rather than forcing men and women to conform to the rigid limits of a formal contract.

Acceptance of these new principles has been most apparent among the young. Much has been made of the increased promiscuity of college and even high school students; of innocent nudity, communal living and coed dorms; and of the conversational freedom and open experimentation that characterize youthful sexuality. However, none of this, historically, is entirely new. As has been amply demonstrated in the memoirs of Virginia Woolf, Lytton Strachey or Isadora Duncan, experimental sexuality has long been accepted among the bohemian, the aristocratic and the eccentric rich. Even in Victorian England there were many who found that "decadence" was certainly fashionable, if not morally acceptable. What has happened, some sociologists believe, is that a number of factors persuaded an unusually large segment of the generation that came of age in the 1960s to accept new behavior patterns. More young people had the time, the money and the inclination to adopt the moral standards that, since the 1920s at least, had been restrained to the Left Banks, Bloomsburys and Greenwich Villages of the world. And the ideas of youth have, as they so often do, filtered through to the rest of the population.

The impact of the sexual revolution varies from country to country in surprising ways. Among Italians, the cult of the virgin is still strong —as recently as 1973, a bridegroom shot his wife on their wedding trip when he concluded that he was not the first man in her life. But when an Italian writer questioned 1,056 mothers and daughters in that same year, she found that sex had become much more significant to women. Only 30 per cent of the mothers considered sex of fundamental im-

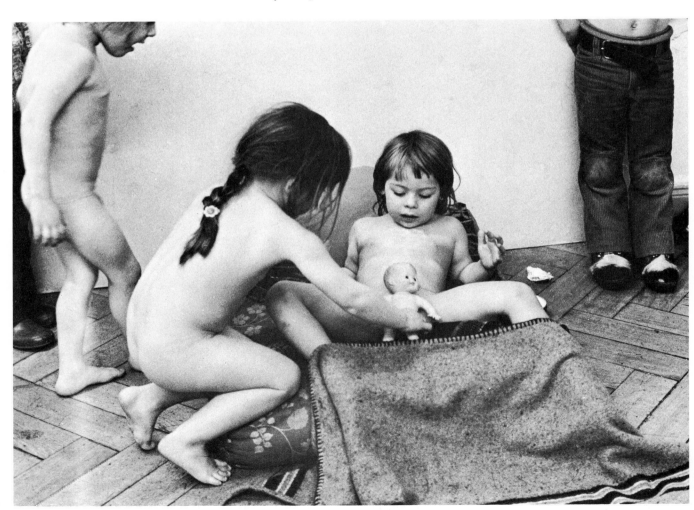

portance in a woman's life; for their daughters, the comparable figure was 93 per cent. And of the older women, just 9 per cent ranked sexual compatibility as the most important factor in marriage; of the younger ones, 66 per cent put sex first.

Given the popular belief that sex practically originated in France, the facts about that country are surprising. It was 1972 before the French did a Kinsey-type study, and even then it was on a far smaller scale. Surveying 2,625 men and women, physician Pierre Simon found that only about half the women between 20 and 29 had had sexual experience before marriage and then usually with their husbands-to-be. Simon shattered the myth of a mistress for every Frenchman; only 30 percent of the husbands he questioned admitted to infidelity. Of the wives, only 10 per cent made the same admission. Moreover, 50 per cent of both men and women said they considered adultery "unforgivable."

Certain significant changes in attitudes toward sex, however, seem to be quite widespread, if not universal. Pornography, for example, is now more generally tolerated than ever before. A broad range of sexual activities is accepted. Homosexuality was legalized in Britain in 1967, and it is no longer considered a "psychiatric disorder" by the American Psychiatric Association. Other sex practices once thought improper are today justified or even encouraged. And education in sexual matters is being revolutionized—for children and for adults as well.

In the United States some 1,500 sex manuals were in print in 1975, and similar books can be bought in every other Western country. In Japan women's magazines publish articles about intercourse illustrated with sketches of sexual positions. The Soviet handbook *Female Sexual Pathology* was so popular when it came out in 1974 that it brought 50 times its listed price, more than girlie magazines smuggled in from Sweden.

Even before adult sex manuals flooded bookshops, the need for better training of children was recognized. The difficulty of getting youngsters to take in the fundamentals is obvious even to parents who have tried their best. Virginia Masters remembers reading about one small boy who listened to various conscientious explanations about a "special place" inside Mummy, and marveled: "In there with all that spinach!" Such alimentary theories are not at all uncommon. Child psychoanalyst Selma Fraiberg tells how four-year-old Debby theorized that the way to have a baby was to eat a watermelon, maybe "a little one and it grows and grows and gets to be big."

Many countries have now made formal sex courses part of the required educational program—but not without controversy. A quarter

In a Berlin kindergarten dedicated to "emancipated education," two four-year-old girls act out a childbirth with a doll. The program seeks to develop happy and unrepressed children, free of hang-ups about sex—but like most such programs, it has met with fierce resistance from conservative parents and educators.

of the secondary schools in France offer sex education, but only 3 per cent of students take the courses. Swedish schools, by contrast, require every child to attend sex education classes beginning in the first grade and continuing through high school. The idea, says Birgitta Linnér, co-founder of the Stockholm Family Counseling Bureau, is to make sure that an aura of guilt and shame never settles over sex. The long-term result, says Linnér, is a "deeper, richer, more meaningful relationship between a man and a woman."

The new morality has brought with it increased tolerance not only for explicit descriptions of sex in educational materials but also for outright pornography with no instructional pretensions. The sale of hardcore pornography to anyone at least 16 years old was legalized in Denmark in 1969. On Copenhagen's elegant pedestrian street *Stroget*, the bluest of blue movie houses can be found not far from the most fashionable shops. In Germany, so-called soft pornography is legal when sold to people at least 18 years old and when not displayed in shops frequented by minors. Moreover, family magazines like *Stern* are free to carry cover photographs of nudes, and they do so often. Japan permits the sale of pornographic magazines (about a thousand are regularly published) as long as they do not include pictures revealing the genitals. In the United States pornography is readily available, although its legal status is not clearly established.

The pornography explosion has been cited by many critics as a detrimental effect of the sexual revolution. Few social scientists agree; they do not think pornography is harmful. In 1970, a United States government commission of behavioral experts concluded that smut is not a cause of crime, delinquency, deviance or emotional disturbance. Twelve of the commission's 18 members said that pornography can actually strengthen conjugal ties. Their finding was based partly on experiments in which married couples watched films and read literature considered hard-core pornography. A majority of the subjects said the experience lowered inhibitions between the partners and made their subsequent sex life more adventurous and pleasurable. In Denmark, whose authorities agree with the U.S. commission, it has been suggested that pornography can actually prevent crime by providing the sexually unstable with a harmless private outlet for their fantasies.

The new permissiveness extends to another, quite different sexual realm, that of erotic behavior among the aged. Especially in the United States, the ancient belief that sexually interested oldsters are either ridiculous or disgusting is disappearing. A 1960 study by G. Newman and C. R. Nichols revealed that 60 per cent of a group of North Carolinians between 60 and 75 were still sexually active, as were 30 per cent of a group over 75. More often than not, the aged who had given up sex had done so because of chronic illness, not out of disinterest. Another investigator, Isadore Rubin, questioned 800 elderly men listed in *Who's Who in America* and found that 70 per cent of those over 65 still engaged in sexual intercourse from one to four times a month. Almost half of those over 75, among them a minister of 92, were still sexually active. In fact, clergymen as a group reported the most activity; editors, publishers and journalists the least.

The recognition of these facts of life have led nursing homes to change their rules. "Up until a few years ago," says Martin Berezin, former president of the Boston Society for Geriatric Psychiatry, "an old couple admitted to a home were separated and their sex life cut off. Now they are more and more being allowed to live together." New marriages after 65 have become common, and retirement communities are the scene of elderly romances. In San Pedro, California, a white-haired grandmother of 57, Regina Shermerhorn, found a joyous relationship

A multilingual, multimedia sex shop flaunts its wares in Copenhagen, where pornography has been legally available to adults since 1969. The effect on sex crimes has been mixed: rates of rape and exhibitionism show little change, while child molestation has decreased sharply. The effect on sales, however, has been clear: according to one pornographer, "Legalization is killing business."

with 72-year-old William Hanson. When she met him, she said, "It was as if I were 17 and had never been on a date. I had never turned anybody on in my life, so far as I knew. Now, all of a sudden, it was Christmas. Believe it or not, we fell in love."

Changes such as these are evidence of a revolution in attitudes—in the general agreement on the way people ought to behave. Whether the revolution extends beyond the "ought to" of attitudes and affects the actuality of behavior is another matter. The repressive beliefs of the Victorians only covered up rampant carnality: adultery was secret but routine; pornography flourished on a huge scale (one famous book, entitled *My Secret Life*, contained 4,200 pages of explicit sexual detail). London supported as many as 120,000 prostitutes, many of them children; and during an eight-year period three hospitals treated 2,700 girls aged 11 to 16 for venereal disease. Today, too, people do not necessarily practice what they preach, and the new permissiveness seems to be more talked about than taken advantage of. Yet there is no doubt that behavior has changed.

The best-documented aspect of the revolution in sexual behavior is the decision of women to take part in sex as a pleasure distinct from procreation. The documentation is simple and reliable: statistics on birth control and abortion. They show that almost everywhere in the world, within the space of a decade or so, women took to sex for pleasure by deliberately preventing its potential for producing children. They did so despite occasional disapproval from men and strong opposition from some religious and governmental bodies. Sweden was the first Western country to liberalize abortion, beginning in 1938. Britain followed in 1967, the United States in 1972, and West Germany and France in 1974. Women took advantage of the changed legal climate. In Britain before 1967, an estimated 100,000 abortions—most illegal—were performed annually; 163,000 were performed in 1974.

Abortion is still almost a last resort, and so the figures on contraceptive use are a more persuasive indicator of the extent to which ordinary women have, as a matter of routine, changed their sex habits. Oral contraceptives—the Pill—first went on sale in 1960, with dramatic results that affected not only the West, but the Orient as well. Eight million women were taking them by 1964, 35 million by 1970, 50 million by 1972. In 1974 some seven million American women were "on the Pill"—about 16 per cent of the country's fertile women. In England 20 per cent of the fertile women were taking it. In Germany 11 million women consumed 2.86 billion pills in 1973. That same year

Japanese women used 390 million, and Chinese women 3.9 billion.

Other, more general, changes in sexual behavior are documented by surveys in many countries. Nearly all establish a continuing trend toward permissiveness. A 1973 study in Lübeck, Germany showed that 79 per cent of the first children born to married couples were conceived before the wedding. Another 1973 poll in Germany, found that 50 per cent of those interviewed thought there was nothing wrong with premarital sex, while another 19 per cent approved of it with reservations. Johns Hopkins University demographers estimated in 1972 that nearly half of all single American girls engaged in sexual activity before they were out of their teens; the situation was thought to be similar in much of the Western world.

For some, such permissiveness has brought more problems than freedom. Social pressure to accept the new morality can be traumatic. One unhappy college freshman told MIT psychotherapist Thomas Cottle, "I don't even have a boy friend. But I had myself fitted for a diaphragm. I had to feel that in some way I was part of it all." For young people not yet emotionally ready for sex, "There is no place to hide, no curfew behind which to take refuge, no rule that can be invoked without loss of face," says child psychoanalyst Ira Mintz. Virgins of both sexes are often suspected, by themselves as well as others, of being sexually inadequate, perhaps even homosexual. If their first attempts at sex are disappointing, as they often are, their fears seem to have been confirmed. Even if they find sex itself enjoyable, they may feel that something is missing. As a young construction worker told Cottle, "Ain't anybody any more knows if he's in love or just turned on."

As a result, some behavioral scientists see signs of reaction toward a new sexual conservatism. Sociologist Ira Reiss predicts that at all age levels, sexual activity may become less compulsive than it seemed in the 1960s and early 1970s. "Living together is going to get more popular, but with an emphasis on stable, two-person relationships," he forecast in 1974. UCLA sociologist Ralph Turner is certain that "marriage is by no means an obsolete institution." About 1970, Turner's students were often militantly opposed to marriage. In 1974 a majority chose marriage as a topic for intensive study.

Whether the sexual relationship will make another pendulum swing all the way back is of course impossible to predict. The revolution of the 20th Century may indeed turn out to be another of many successive shifts in morality. But no one today can doubt that he has lived through a revolution—and witnessed one of the most remarkable transformations of behavior in all human history.

In the eye of the beholder

Neither a bikinied Frenchwoman nor the painted Xicrin girl at right is likely to realize it, but her sex appeal is largely imaginary. All the many ways men and women try to heighten their attractiveness for the opposite sex, says psychologist Arthur H. Feiner, involve "the capacity to evoke fantasy." Such fantasy, he notes, "is evoked by the short skirts worn by girls as they walk down the street. It has little to do with the shapeliness of the legs, or the class of the woman, but with the spirit of sexual receptiveness conveyed by her . . . dress." Clothes are indeed often designed to arouse such a spirit, and the allure of the miniskirt has its equivalent in other societies: in India, where men admire hips and abdomens, women's outfits often leave the midriff bare.

But clothes are only one means of evoking the fantasy of attraction. Both decorations and makeup are especially elaborate in those societies where near-nudity is the norm. In the Central Highlands of New Guinea, tribesmen go courting in headdresses of eagle and cockatoo feathers, their faces painted with charcoal and powdered pigment, grease rubbed on their bodies, shells inserted in their noses and strips of fur bound around their foreheads.

Body movement is another important part of physical appeal—Marilyn Monroe's walk helped make her the sex symbol of her time. Because dance is based on body movement, it is often a means by which the sexes try to impress each other erotically; the graceful swaying of European waltzers no less than the languid hip-swinging of Polynesians or the gyrations of Africans *(pages 138-139)* is aimed at the universal objective: attraction.

Undergoing a beauty treatment, a girl of Brazil's Xicrin tribe is adorned with a dark-blue dye made from the jenipapo fruit—its juices stain the skin for at least two weeks. Without their body paint, members of the tribe consider themselves as unappealingly naked as Westerners would without their clothes.

A transparent veil partially conceals an Indian Muslim's face while enhancing her beauty.

Clothes that make the man—and woman

To attract the girls, a Tahitian wears a bold-colored pareau and a flowered garland.

Silk was invented so that women could go naked in clothes, according to an ancient Arabian comment on the subtly revealing clothes that Orientals still wear today. Modern psychologists endorse this analysis. They maintain that clothing has a purpose that transcends mere warmth, for both men and women. It accentuates their good features and conceals their defects, thereby enhancing individual attractiveness.

In Western countries, men show little of their bodies but exaggerate their musculature with padding and tailoring. Clothes can also serve as a substitute for an appealing physical appearance—a gaily colored and eye-catching dress on a plain woman will gain her the male attention she would not otherwise elicit.

The waists and bustlines of these Balinese women are emphasized by the wide cummerbunds that are wrapped tightly around their filmy blouses.

An American girl slips off her bolero to reveal a low-cut halter that bares her shoulders and back.

Prettying up for the opposite sex

*A Brazilian Indian sports
face paint of fruit seeds and oil.*

*The scars that this woman from Cameroon in west
Africa wears on her face were put there as beauty marks.*

*Strings of shells hanging from a larger
shell enclose this New Guinean's nose.*

Most Western women use makeup to enhance the appeal of their own features. But in some cultures—most notably in Africa, South America and the Pacific islands—facial decoration is employed by men and women to create wholly new and artificial patterns with mud plaster, tattoos, paint and even scars.

Grotesque as such images may appear to outsiders, they all serve the same purpose as any other makeup: attracting the opposite sex. The geometric patterns painted on the faces of girls in Africa's Gueré tribe at puberty signal that the girls are being instructed in sex by the older women. Aware that the makeup attracts the men, the girls taunt any they happen to meet, in much the same way that Western youngsters wearing their first lipstick are emboldened to flirt with the boys.

*Mascara, eyeliner and lipstick underscore
the beauty of a young Italian woman.*

134

A line down the nose of this girl from the San Blas Islands, Panama, produces an appealing elongation.

Reddish earth paint made from baked clay encrusts the face of a New Guinea Highlander.

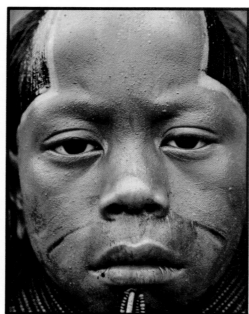

A New Guinea girl dusts her hair and tattooed cheeks with powder.

To accentuate his youth, a Brazilian Indian shaves his forehead and wears a lip plug.

The clay-painted design on the face of this Ivory Coast girl shows she is of marriageable age.

135

The anatomy of feminine allure

Almost any part of a woman's body can be enticing to a man, but in every culture certain parts are thought to be more stimulating than others. Protruding buttocks make a girl desirable to the Masai of East Africa; among the Mangaians of Polynesia, wide hips are deemed attractive. Body proportion is also important; while Europeans and Americans admire slimness, Eskimos equate beauty with stoutness.

Within a society, fashions change and attention shifts from one part to another. Thus, Western man's turn-of-the-century obsession with well-turned ankles gave way, after skirt lengths were raised, to an interest in legs generally. An exception to the rule of change is the bosom: it was as much admired in Classical Rome as it is today.

The nape of the neck, here exposed by the low collar of a kimono, has long been an enticement for Japanese men.

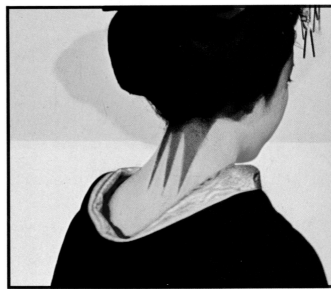

A bikini on an American girl reveals more than it conceals of the breasts and hips liked by Westerners.

In India, where long hair is seductive, this young woman's lustrous mane is enhanced by flowers.

The eyes of traditionally garbed Iranian women like this one are their only unveiled feature—a provocative lure to their countrymen.

The invitation of the dance

Dancing to attract the opposite sex is such a basic part of nature that gooney birds, ostriches, spiders and people all over the world do it. Among the humans, Polish men show off for the girls with spectacular folk-dance leaps, Romanian girls charm the men with their slow, graceful steps, and in Spain both sexes strut in flamenco dancing.

Dances in which male and female perform for each other have a lengthy tradition. In the 18th Century, couples bowed and curtsied their way through the minuet. By the early 20th Century, such stately displays had given way to the Charleston and, 40 years later, to the "twist." Today the style persists in the isolated patterns of rock dancing *(far right)*, which allow each of the partners to display erotic movements to the other.

Changing Times

5

Karen and Bob Maness of St. Louis, Missouri, were married in 1966, when she was 16 and he was 21. Eventually, one of them became a police officer. The other got a job as a service representative for the telephone company while shouldering most of the responsibility for keeping house and bringing up the couple's two daughters. The family's way of life seems ordinary enough, except for one fact: Karen was the police officer and Bob the service representative. "I would never go back to doing all the housework. I would never go back to a traditional role for a woman," Karen told an interviewer, and Bob nodded his head in agreement. But their unconventional life style was not so troublefree as it appeared to outsiders or as the couple themselves wanted to believe. Just one month after they had been interviewed, the Manesses filed for divorce.

Their experience tells a lot about the places of men and women in recent decades. As the century moved into its final quarter, changes were occurring that scarcely would have seemed possible only a few years before. Women were moving out of the home and into professions and jobs that previously had been the exclusive domain of men. In increasing numbers, women such as India's Indira Gandhi *(left)* were getting elected to high political offices formerly held by men—in Mrs. Gandhi's case to a position previously occupied by her own father, Jawaharlal Nehru.

Men were also caught up in the change in growing numbers. They were being forced to rethink their cherished beliefs about marriage, home life and the working world. They have had to take on responsibilities for emotional support and encouragement of women, and to modify their own roles accordingly. And often they were finding themselves washing dishes, baby-sitting, cooking, cleaning house—and competing with women for jobs and raises.

Few men and women went so far as the Manesses of St. Louis and attempted a nearly complete reversal of the conventional male and female roles in marriage. But even those who made far more modest experiments found that the process of change is always difficult, and that while the possibilities for different role behavior are great, they are not unlimited. And yet there could be no doubt that great social forces were at work everywhere in the world and would continue to alter the lives of people in almost all cultures.

The impetus for the big change came, of course, from women. It was they who were giving vent to their dissatisfaction and they whose status and roles were most directly affected. Thus the dimensions of the changes that have altered—and are continuing to alter—the relationships between the sexes are best indicated by what has happened to women. They have come a long way. The improvement in their status vis-a-vis men is directly measurable in a number of areas. New laws have been passed and old ones repealed to free them of old restrictions and give them rights long reserved for men. They have secured a measure of economic independence by taking jobs—in the United States almost half the adult women work—and gaining income they can truly call their own. Not only do they work, but more of them work at good jobs, winning stimulating, satisfying careers and high posts in business and the professions. Although the number of women in high positions is still small compared to the number of men, the increase in their representation over past decades is dramatic. Perhaps most important of all, women have won respect. Attitudes toward them have changed and are continuing to change. The day when women could be considered second-class human beings is, if not gone, at least fast ending.

One measure of the improvement in the status of women is found by looking in the lawbooks. In almost all of the countries of the world, the changes are significant. While old laws scarcely acknowledged the existence of women as anything more than chattels—or at best as children—new statutes recognize them as responsible and independent adults.

This fundamental recognition of a basic right has come exceedingly slowly and often grudgingly. American, British and Swedish women could not vote in general elections until the end of World War I; Japanese, French and Italian women had to wait until World War II was over. In the United States, dozens of laws now prohibit sex discrimination in employment, politics and personal freedoms. In Britain, the Sex Disqualification Act of 1919, along with a few other laws, makes women legally equal to men in most respects: They can hold any office, enter any profession, make business contracts, sue and be sued. In West

Germany, a 1957 law assures women the right to manage their own property, to share in decisions about property jointly owned in marriage and to inherit half of a husband's estate.

French women have not done so well in many areas. Their subordinate place is in part a hangover from the Napoleonic Code of 1804. "Napoleon detested women, except for one particular use," explained Françoise Giroud, minister for women's affairs in the government of Valéry Giscard d'Estaing. It was not until 1938 that France repealed the article requiring women to obey their husbands; it was 1965 before the law permitted them to open bank accounts without their husbands' permission and it was 1969 before they finally won the right to buy contraceptives. In the mid-1970s, a French husband could not be convicted of adultery unless he moved his mistress into his house, whereas his wife's adultery was an offense no matter what the circumstances. In some areas, however, French women have enjoyed surprising freedom —for one thing, the French have been more ready than most people in the West to accept women in responsible positions in the professions.

The women of Japan have just begun to emerge from a state of submission and almost total dependence on their husbands. For many centuries after a period of relative independence *(page 16)*, their lives were shackled by a Confucian moral code that required every female to obey her parents when she was young, her husband after her marriage and her sons in old age. The women's subordinate status was spelled out in the law. No woman could inherit; if there were no male descendants, family property went to the oldest daughter's husband. Change came only at the end of World War II, when Japan's new constitution guaranteed equality of the sexes. But old attitudes die hard. A 1947 statute permitted potential heirs to renounce their inheritance rights, and for years after, close to twice as many daughters as sons chose to do just that, and so did about 70 times as many wives as husbands. The ideal Japanese woman was still self-sacrificing, demure and retiring; it was 1970 before that ideal had begun to disappear.

Statute books and official constitutions, however, tend to reflect the objectives of a society rather than its actual performance in accomplishing its aims. This fact applies with special force to the status of women around the world. A better indicator of their true situation is jobs—the number they hold, the kind that are available to them, the money they receive in exchange for their labor and the reasons they take them. Women began working at outside jobs as soon as there were factories to work in. But the mill girls were mostly young, unmarried and poor. Proportionately, they made up a small part of the total working population.

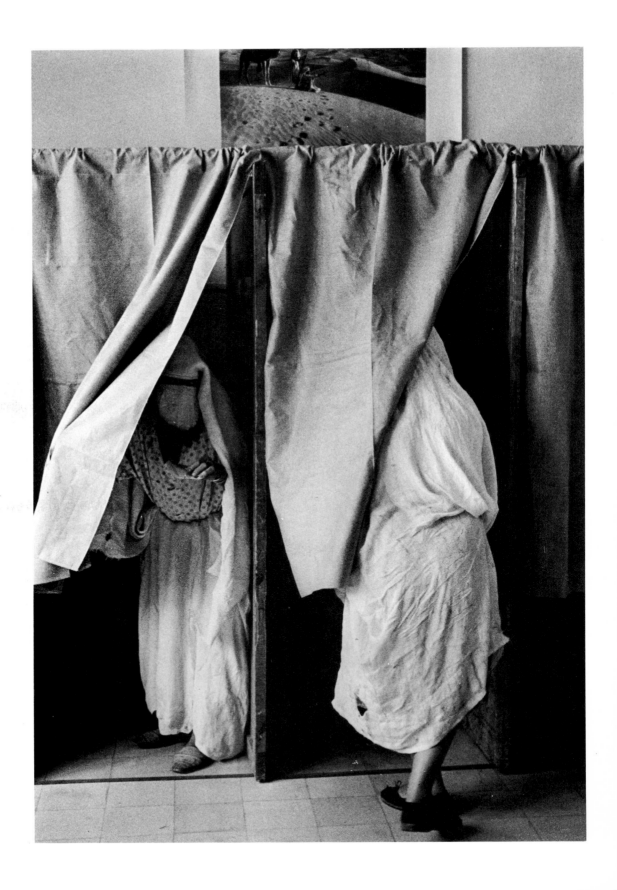

Today the percentage of women in the work force is much higher almost everywhere.

In Japan the number of working women has been rising steadily and today accounts for about 40 per cent of all employed persons. In Europe, too, more and more women work. Even in Italy, where the shortage of jobs is so acute that millions of men have been forced to move to other countries in search of work, women make up more than a quarter of the labor force. In Britain, France and West Germany, about 40 per cent of all employees are female.

More detailed statistics are available for the United States, enough to provide a profile of the American woman and to suggest some ramifications of her changed status. In 1975, around 45 per cent of the female population held jobs. The number of women entering the labor force was rising faster than the number of men: between 1963 and 1973 the number of working women rose by 40 per cent, while the number of working men was rising by only 15 per cent.

That so many women held paying jobs at all was a remarkable development. But a more significant fact emerges from analysis of the figures. For the kind of woman who worked had changed. For a long time unmarried women had been expected to take jobs—after all, they were expected to help support themselves. (The young women recently out of school were assumed to be looking for husbands. The other single women were pitied because they had not found a husband to support them.) But in years past a wife who worked was a mark of shame either to herself or to her husband. She shamed herself if she liked to work—she was considered an "unnatural" wife and mother who did not want to be at home. She shamed her husband if she worked for the money—she was being forced to take on a masculine duty because he was not a "good provider" for his family. These attitudes seem largely to have disappeared, at least among some segments of the population, and not only in the United States but in several countries. In France about 60 per cent of the working women are married. In the United States the proportion is similar. And there the average employed female is past 40 years of age; two out of five are mothers, and 40 per cent of them have children six years old or younger.

These studies indicate that women share with their husbands the task of supporting their families. When women in the United States were asked why they work, an astonishing 85 per cent replied that they need the money. For some, the need is unqualified; one out of 10 U.S. families was headed by a woman in 1971. But the majority of working women do not have this absolute need. A high proportion of them have working husbands and are not poverty-stricken. The percentage of women from middle and upper economic levels who work is higher than that representing the lower levels. The figures are astonishing. In 1974 in families with incomes over $10,000, there were 30 million working women; in families with incomes less than $10,000, the number of working women was 14.5 million. Even in families with annual incomes over $20,000, there were 9.2 million working women.

These women obviously do not work to forestall starvation. The money they bring in lifts their families still higher on the economic ladder, and some authorities believe they made possible the affluence of the '60s and early '70s, in effect paying for college education for their children, new homes and vacation trips for their families. Some of them made major financial contributions: one out of four working wives brought home more than 40 per cent of her family's total income. There is another way of looking at this same statistic, however, and it suggests another aspect of the change in women's behavior. While one out of four working wives contributed 40 per cent of family income, half of

them contributed only 20 per cent or less. Even that increment helped to improve their living standards. Yet it is small enough to indicate that for many women, the expressed need for money only partially explained why they worked. To them, a job provided intellectual stimulation, the opportunity to meet people, escape from household drudgery, pride in work well done and a feeling of independence. Their earnings became, to some extent, the token of respect that the modern society bestows on anyone who holds a paying job.

The statistics on working women establish one important change in the relationship between the sexes. No longer must the woman stay home to cook and tend children while the man goes out to earn their living; today both are accepted as integral parts of their society's economic life. That fact, however, does not mean that the male's traditional domination in economics has ended. Women may work in vastly larger numbers, but they still work mostly at lesser jobs than men do, and they almost always earn less money.

On the average, American working women in the mid-1970s earned about 60 per cent of what was paid to men. Moreover, according to the Joint Economic Committee of the U.S. Congress, the gap was widening. In England, West Germany and France, the pay discrepancy was similar. Even when women were doing the same work as men, one study in the United States showed that they were paid 20 per cent less—in violation of a law requiring equal pay for equal work. In another study, University of Michigan researchers calculated the dollars-and-cents cost of sexism. They began by rating the jobs of 351 women and 695 men on the basis of prestige and degree of responsibility required. Then they graded the jobholders on their educational level, their past experience and their seniority with their employers. Adding up the job and personal ratings, they found that 95 per cent of the women were earning less than men with the same rating. The average difference came to $3,500, but one woman was underpaid by some $12,000.

The basic reason for women's pay disadvantage, however, remains the blunt fact that most of them hold comparatively low-level jobs—even in the professions women's careers are restricted. In 1970 the majority of working women in the United States were employed in the same five fields in which most women had been employed in 1920: they were maids, kindergarten or elementary school teachers, nurses, sales clerks or office workers. Through no choice of their own, many women were crowded into vocational ghettos in which they were doing work that offered relatively little chance for advancement, since men held most of the managerial posts.

Mothers in India, intent upon freeing themselves from the unwanted pregnancies that women have borne for centuries, listen as a doctor describes an intrauterine contraceptive device. Women's participation in family-planning programs is credited for a sharp drop in India's birth rate: from 41 per 1,000 people in 1968 to 35 per 1,000 in 1974.

147

*Demanding pay for tending hearth and home, some
housewives in Italy stage a demonstration in
Rome in 1962 seeking a government pension at age
55. The next year the parliament passed a pension
plan, although women had to be 65 before
they could start collecting the benefits from it.*

Very often there seems to be a direct relationship between the number of underpaid, monotonous jobs in a field and the number of women who work in that field. One example is the electronics industry. Initially, it needed technically trained workers and hired mostly men. Now it requires many unskilled employees to assemble components. Apparently as a result, the number of women in the electronics industry jumped 82 per cent between 1950 and 1965 in the United States, 73 per cent over a similar period in France and 313 per cent in West Germany during the 1950s. Communications is another field with no lack of boring jobs. More than 80 per cent of all the telephone operators in Germany are women, while in France and the United States, the figure is greater than 90 per cent.

Women have made some gains in business and industry. A survey of 20 major United States corporations showed that although women held fewer than 1 per cent of the top-level positions, growing numbers of them are sitting on boards of directors and occupying key executive positions in many corporations.

In the professions, the picture is mixed but generally improving for women. Medicine is a good example. In 1974, only about 10 per cent of American doctors were women, but 23 per cent of the country's first-year medical students were female, and the proportion was expected to go up in succeeding years. Some 12 per cent of French doctors were women, as were some 20 per cent of British doctors. At the head of the list was the Soviet Union, where women made up 70 per cent of the profession. Admittedly, medicine is less prestigious in Russia than elsewhere, but it is nevertheless a striking fact that the Soviet Union had more female surgeons, medical specialists and hospital directors than all of Western Europe put together.

In the realm of higher education, the percentage of faculty women is also rising. In the decade after 1964 the number of women on the faculties of American colleges and universities increased by 4 per cent, but more important, the posts they held were more prestigious than formerly. Once it was almost a rule that when two graduate students married, the man eventually became a professor while his wife resigned herself to being a research assistant. No more. One reason is that the United States government now insists that any institution getting more than $50,000 a year in federal grants take "affirmative action" to give women an equal opportunity for the better jobs. Many colleges have relaxed nepotism rules that formerly prohibited them from employing both husband and wife; Bennington College in 1972 named Gail Parker as president and her husband Thomas as vice president. The

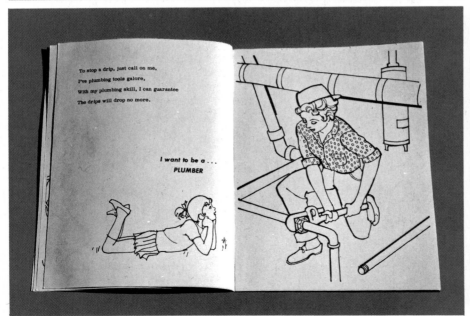

Spreading around the world in the early 1970s, the feminist movement pressed its demands for women's rights in every imaginable medium

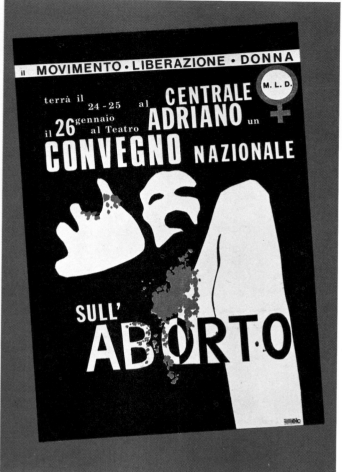

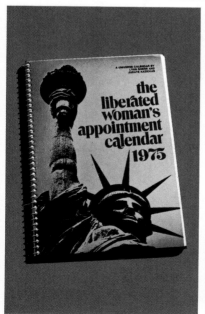

from comic strips to campaign buttons and, in the bottom row, matchbooks and a French proabortion T-shirt saying, "My body is my own."

University of Kansas tries to find couples who want to work together, and a few institutions, among them Stanford and Hamline, look for husband-and-wife teams who will share one teaching position.

The situation in law is also changing rapidly. Women constituted 3 per cent of U.S. lawyers in 1974, but they accounted for 22 per cent of entering law students. Twenty per cent of the French lawyers were women, as were 6 per cent of the profession in Britain and 35 per cent in the Soviet Union. Even Japan has seen a change. In 1974 two women became the first of their sex in that country to be appointed to the Japanese High Court. "Twenty years ago I was a pioneer. These days there are few obstacles for women," said one of them, Aiko Noda.

The most spectacular gains for women, however, have been made in politics. Ironically, history's most influential female leaders —from Livia, Cleopatra, Elizabeth I and Catherine the Great to Indira Gandhi—have ruled over cultures that have long traditions of repressing women, and the great Western democracies, where all people are supposed by ideology to be equal, have traditionally remained cool to the very idea of female rule. But in 1975, Margaret Thatcher became head of the Conservative Party in Britain and thus a potential Prime Minister. In one year in the United States, 1974, Ella Grasso was elected governor of Connecticut, Mary Anne Krupsak won office as lieutenant governor of New York and March Fong was chosen secretary of state in California. Janet Gray Hayes became mayor of San José, California, the first of her sex to win that office in a city of more than half a million people, and Susie Sharp of North Carolina was the first woman to be elected chief justice of a state supreme court.

New opportunities for women are also opening up in fields that have always been male preserves. In Japan, Midori Sato operates a detective agency that employs 30 people, including her own husband, and is so well thought of that the Emperor retained her to investigate the young woman Crown Prince Akihito wanted to marry. (Mrs. Sato approved.) In the United States, Carol Jean Bain became a coal miner in West Virginia, Judith Ann Neuffer of Ohio won an assignment to train to be the first woman in the Navy to work as a pilot, and Wilma Schneider and Bonni Briggs were hired as guards at the San Quentin prison in California. Surprisingly, in view of the stereotype of women as the weaker sex, active police work attracts a startling number of female recruits. Of course, policewomen in America have been performing clerical and other inside tasks for many years, but the assignment of women to regular police beats got underway only in the late 1960s. In 1972 there were about 45 policewomen on patrol duty in the United States; by 1975 the total had risen to 2,000.

In the old days when job opportunities were severely limited, most women automatically thought of marriage as their life's work. But the new career opportunities and the new attitudes toward work have prompted a new ordering of priorities. Women are no longer leaping into marriage. A 1974 study, based on interviews with 239 experts in religion, psychology and psychiatry, along with 384 average men and women in 43 American cities, reported that women were marrying later than they used to. "The old pressure to get married fast is dead," said Sally Durwald, a counselor at the University of Wisconsin.

Another bit of evidence of the altered attitude comes from a survey of Vassar College alumnae. Most of those who graduated in the mid-'50s wanted marriage more than anything else in life, with a career taking second place—if it figured at all in their plans. The mid-'60s graduates, however, insisted that with or without marriage, they needed a career to be fulfilled. Early in the '70s, Boston psychoanalyst Jacob Swartz noted that more women than in the past were "actively considering a single life as an alternative" to marriage. Only a few years earlier Simone de Beauvoir had written, "Most women are married, or have been, or plan to be, or suffer from not being."

Those women who do marry expect their husbands to take their wives' job aspirations and careers seriously. In a few cases, the husband may even sacrifice his job and move to another city so that his wife can advance her education or career. William Selleck, a professor of English at California State University at Pomona, resigned in 1972 when IBM promoted his wife to a job in Denver. He agreed to move again in 1974 because his wife was offered yet another promotion, this one calling for a transfer to Minneapolis. Until recently employers rarely asked women to move from city to city. For one thing, their female workers were mostly clerks. Besides, managers usually assumed that women with families would refuse transfers and that offers of promotion to another city would do nothing but stir up family conflict. "There has been a dramatic change on both sides," says James Crain, an assistant vice president of the New England Telephone and Telegraph Company. "We're making offers we wouldn't have thought we could make ten years ago, and women are saying they are flexible."

The new attitudes of women toward work, marriage and family responsibilities are reflected by shifts in the behavior of men. These changes are less well-publicized than those directly affecting women, but they are widespread.

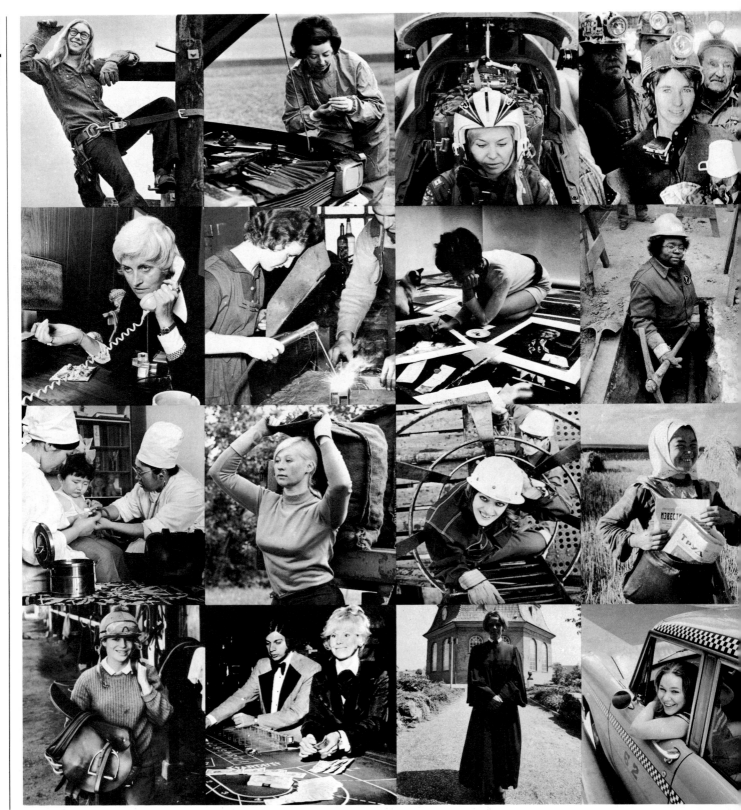

Women in jobs that once went mostly to men are now a familiar sight. In the top row are a German airline pilot and an American sports

official. The second row includes a French boat captain, the third an English coal deliverer, the fourth a Swedish construction worker.

More and more men are helping their wives with household chores, especially when the wives are mothers who work outside the home. The need for cooperation is great; according to the United Nations, working mothers around the world average less than two thirds the free time available to their husbands—they must continue with family duties in addition to their jobs. Infrequently, husbands and wives agree to take turns at home tasks on a regular 50-50 schedule. In one U.S. family the parents share the housework so evenly that their six-year-old daughter was at first surprised when she saw, in her unliberated school primer, a picture of a mother cooking and a father reading his paper. "Why is she working and he's just sitting there?" she asked. Then she answered her own question. "I know. It must be her week to cook."

While husbands pitch in with housework more often than they used to, few have gone so far as to switch roles completely. For all the women in roles that were previously held only by men, there are few men in female ones. "I don't think there are a dozen men in the United States who could survive a year as house-husbands," says Warren Farrell of Brooklyn College. One of the dozen is Phillip Rabinowitz of Brighton, Massachusetts. He kept house and took care of his infant son while his wife attended law school. He did not find it easy: "I can't wait to get out of the house and back to work. I love my son Adam, but I can see how taking care of a kid can drive a woman up the wall."

Dividing the tasks at home is the key problem for married couples who feel that the woman should be working and getting more out of life. Husbands like Phillip Rabinowitz, who will remain at home while their wives go to school or support the family, are presently so rare that their very existence is the subject of magazine articles and television interviews, and even those men who share the burden equally are still comparatively few. In the great majority of cases it is the wife who cares for the children. And as long as one sex has to bear the main responsibility for raising children, it is bound to remain at a competitive disadvantage in the vocational marketplace, and equality will continue to be an elusive goal.

In the long run the greatest single obstacle for women who want to work or upgrade their jobs may well be the patterns of child rearing. In the United States, for example, working mothers typically spend their first years on the job in training positions, leave to have children in their late twenties—just when the average male is seeking out his first major promotion—and then return to the work force once all their children are in school. Day care centers, to look after preschool children while their mothers worked, would relieve some of this pressure but

this solution seems remote in the U.S. Although a quarter of all American mothers with children under six also hold jobs, only 2 per cent of the children of working mothers are in group day care programs. Very young children are watched by relatives or servants; older ones may be left to fend for themselves.

Learning a skill more often taught to girls, a four-year-old boy in a nursery school in San Francisco plies one needle while a helpful teacher threads another. Since school policy allows pupils to pick any subject that is attractive to them, this youngster could decide for himself what he wanted to try his hand at. He chose needlework.

European day care systems are much more extensive than those in the United States, and the length of paid maternity leave is, in some countries, controlled by legislation. Such programs may account, in part, for the greater participation of European women in the more competitive professions. But many female workers in Europe are also likely to drop out of the work force while their children are young and to return later in low-level or part-time jobs.

The only place the pattern differs is in the Communist countries of Europe. There, women return to work after maternity leave, delegating the care of their babies to day care centers or relatives, but then they retire earlier than men. Having completed their careers at the age of 50 or so, many of these women turn to caring for the children of their own

*A baseball pitcher who also hit a home
run to win the game, eight-year-old Nancy
Lotsey enjoys the boys' admiration after
her first game with the Morristown, New
Jersey, Small Fry League—which earlier
had refused her application to play.*

daughters and sons. Some women in Eastern Europe, however, have recently begun to press for permission to retire five years later in exchange for the right to take five years off at an earlier stage to stay home with their children until they are old enough for school.

Governmental action can simplify the lives of working women simply by establishing new rules for maternity leaves and retirement and by setting up centers for child care. A few steps in that direction have been taken. But official measures are insufficient. They can be impeded or even negated by informal resistance—some from women themselves, but probably most from men. A number of behavioral scientists maintain that certain features of the current relationship between the sexes are fixed—unavoidably locked into their behavioral inheritances. And if anything can be gathered from history, it is that those who are in power are not likely to be willing to give up their privileges. When freer female sexuality seemed to be a major goal of the women's liberationists, the movement was more popular with men, but the recent emphasis on social and vocational, as well as sexual, equality has encountered serious opposition. Legislation that requires the hiring of more women—on college faculties or in industry—has called forth legal challenges on the grounds that it discriminates against men.

So far, few working women have directly threatened men. Most of them work in "women's" jobs or fields. Even those who have advanced have rarely done so by displacing men. Beyond job competition, however, men's resistance to female equality probably rises from deeper and less obvious motives. For if the roles of men and women are to be fundamentally altered, society's view of manliness must change as radically as its view of femininity has already been altered. Given the traditional definition of the role of men in Western cultures, this change is bound to be regarded by many men as a threat.

The old definition of masculinity seems remarkably intact. What makes a man a man is still, for most people, a combination of strength and will. He is admired for his mastery over nature, his audacity and his grace under pressure. The challenge of competition and the respect for power still are key motivating forces. The old images of manliness retain their appeal: the suppression of emotion, the hard-nosed ability to make decisions without sentiment and the stiff upper lip that makes masculine authority felt.

Such male characteristics are curiously dependent on the secondary role of women. If men must be stoic and brave, fight wars, slay dragons and stay late at the office, then women, out of gratitude at least, should remain emotional, seductive and soft. The front-line troops need support;

they look to women to provide it. The liberation of women removes many props from the old foundations of masculinity. If women are to be self-sufficient there is little reason for men to be steely-eyed and protective, and even less for women to comfort them. Thus, if women are to graduate from their traditional role as the weaker sex, men must relinquish their role as the stronger one. Such a reshaping of outlook requires far more than persuading men to help with the dinner dishes or to take a turn at house-cleaning. It involves the basic elements of which entire cultures are built.

In the mid-'70s, it looked as if society would eventually arrive at some new definitions of masculinity and femininity. No one could predict with certainty what the definitions would be, but chances were that at least some of the traditional distinctions between the sexes would continue to seem important. Even in egalitarian Israel, women place a high value on old-fashioned feminine accomplishments. When psychologist Tamar Breznitz-Svidovsky studied Israeli women during and after the Yom Kippur war of 1973, she found Golda Meir to be an anomaly, not a typical representative of her countrywomen. Most Israeli women, the researcher found, cared more about such homemaking activities as knitting, sewing and baking than about making themselves useful in public life. And although Israeli women have long been liable to military conscription, when Breznitz-Svidovsky asked her subjects if they thought members of their sex should join combat units in wartime, the women said no, that fighting was unfeminine.

Before women can achieve full equality with men, the attitudes not just of men but of all society must be modified. There seems to be no biological necessity that prevents young women from becoming surgeons, locomotive drivers or presidents of multinational corporations, but the social evaluation of the woman's role is not so easily altered. The roles society deems proper often are slower to change in people's minds than the realities they describe. If people believe that women do not have to work, it is hard to convince them that day care centers deserve high priority. If people have little experience with female doctors, they more easily assume that women are naturally ill-equipped for the task.

A major effort to combat this kind of role stereotyping has been underway in the United States. One facet concentrates on the elimination of sexism from textbooks and school curricula. The idea is to let youngsters grow up feeling that they can be what they want to be, and to prevent the educational system from conditioning them to expect the world to be tilted in favor of males.

The reformers discovered surprising examples of sex bias in the text-

Homecoming Queen David Mosher is crowned in a ceremony at the University of California at Davis. Running on a platform that sexist contests for homecoming queens should be abolished, Mosher beat out seven women students.

books they examined. An analysis of 2,760 stories in 134 books found two and a half times as many stories about boys as about girls. These books suggested 147 career possibilities for boys, while mentioning only 26—mothers, nurses, librarians and the like—for girls. Moreover, the male characters seemed to have a monopoly on personality traits considered desirable in late 20th Century America. Other investigators make the same charges. One example they cite is a fourth-grade reader that has a girl saying, "Oh, Raymond, boys are much braver than girls." Another is a primer in which a smug little boy says of his sister: "She can not skate. Look at her, Mother. She is just like a *girl*. She gives up." Some feminists have fought the battle of the books in the courts. The feminists' argument: Since a federal statute bans sex discrimination in educational programs that get money from the United States treasury, and since the federal government helps pay for textbooks used by local school boards, the use of sexist books breaks U.S. law.

Such pressure has brought reform. In California, the legislature passed a law forbidding the use of sex-biased materials in public schools. At least two major American publishers require authors and editors to treat the sexes evenly in school texts: Both must be depicted as having "*human* strengths and weaknesses." Thus traits like boldness, initiative and assertiveness, traditionally considered masculine virtues, are to be praised in women as well as in men, while gentleness, compassion and sensitivity, once thought of as feminine qualities, are to be portrayed as admirable in both sexes. The publishers' guidelines ban any implication in children's books that "all women have a mother instinct or the emotional life of a family suffers because a woman works." Sometimes, says one directive, "The man should be shown preparing the meals, doing the laundry or diapering the baby, while the woman builds bookcases or takes out the trash."

A number of American school systems have dropped the barriers that used to keep some children out of traditionally sex-linked courses. In New Milford, Connecticut, all sixth-year students, the boys as well as the girls, are required to study home economics for one semester and industrial arts for another. After experiencing both kinds of work, the children are allowed to choose to pursue either in later courses.

In the long run, education probably will be the most effective force in establishing an equitable balance between the sexes. For generations are now being brought up that no longer subscribe to the old stereotypes. The behavioral changes that were initiated in the '60s and '70s are still gathering momentum, and only history will be able to say how profound their effect will be on the relationships of men and women.

A thoroughly modern marriage

Jean and Françoise Kerleroux were married in 1963, before the social revolution of the 1960s and '70s began to transform the life styles of men and women. Moreover, Jean and Françoise are French, and social change comes about slowly in traditionbound France. There, most wives are expected to stay home, fill the roles of housekeeper and mother and practice a subservience to their husbands that has been likened to the relationship of a nun to a cardinal.

Given that tradition, the couple's marriage got off to an awkward start. Jean was a struggling cartoonist earning little. Françoise supported the family teaching—and also did housework and later took care of the baby, Pauline. A second child, Julie, forced a change. Although outside help eventually lightened home chores, Françoise could not keep up with the domestic duties in addition to her outside work. Jean, normally at home all day drawing, agreed to help. Despite the ingrained ideas of masculinity that have given men a special place in French society, the couple tried to readjust their relationship along more equal lines.

By the time a third daughter, Elisa, was born, Jean was sharing child care and housework, and his assumption of traditionally feminine duties enabled Françoise to make a career as a university scholar and teacher. The transformation of their marriage has been difficult, understandably more for Jean than for Françoise. Their individual freedom has inevitably lessened a mutual dependence he prizes. Yet even after Jean became a successful cartoonist and the family's principal breadwinner, he and Françoise clung to their modern approach to marriage.

Françoise dictates the weekly grocery list to Jean, who does the family shopping. He took on many of the traditionally feminine household chores, while she assumed many organizational and financial duties usually a husband's.

PHOTOGRAPHED BY RICHARD KALVAR

Françoise (left) discusses new books on linguistics with a friend, Danielle Godard, who is also a linguistics teacher.

At home in the evening, Françoise prepares for a lecture while Elisa finishes supper. Though Jean agreed to cook for the children, preparing the adults' dinner remained Françoise's job.

A wife far from the kitchen

As a little girl, Françoise was smart and ambitious. She wanted a family when she grew up, but she also wanted a life of her own. She became not only a wife and mother, but also a linguistics teacher at Nanterre University near Paris.

A graduate student was engaged to help with chores when the children were home from school and day-care nursery. But Françoise and Jean settled on an arrangement for splitting the housework. Françoise, in addition to helping care for the children, assumed all responsibility for family sewing and for cooking for Jean and herself. Because Jean has an aversion to filling out forms, Françoise also agreed to handle duties performed by many husbands —paying the bills and making out tax reports and social security forms.

Françoise explains a point to one of the classes she teaches each week. Though she may be in the classroom only one and a half days, preparing the lectures might take as many as 25 hours a week.

Life at home with father

When Jean was a small boy, his father, a member of the French resistance, was killed by the Nazis. At the age of eight Jean found himself in charge of the family. It was a role he detested, but the experience of looking out for his two younger brothers may have made it easier for him, after his marriage, to accept the traditionally female jobs. He assumed responsibility not only for shopping, but for helping with cooking and dressing the children—while putting in a full day's work drawing.

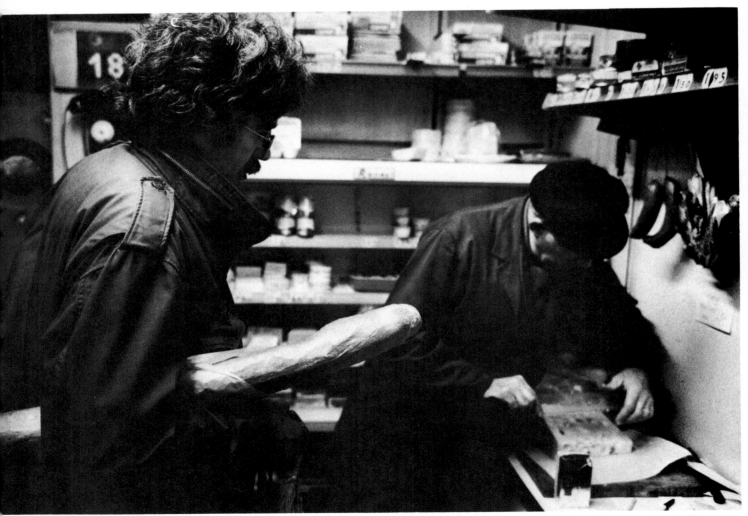

Jean, a loaf of bread under his arm, waits for the cheese that will complete the grocery shopping list made out earlier by Françoise.

Frowning in concentration, Jean works on one of his political drawings. After years of struggle, he eventually became established as one of France's best known —and best paid—political cartoonists.

Jean vacuums his work area on a weekend. The new division of daily tasks still left Françoise with the chores of organizing meals, arranging closets and keeping track of the girls' clothes.

Pauline (foreground) and Julie wait while Jean fixes breakfast. Sometimes he rebelled, saying that Françoise should do the housework. But deep down, she felt, he accepted the justice of sharing.

167

Satisfying times together

Because Jean and Françoise took up separate roles and separate lives, they made a deliberate effort to join in family experiences. Each was prepared to discipline the children—though it was Jean who proved more effective at it —and both romped with the girls in the evenings and helped the older ones with their homework. And on weekends all five might go to a family cottage in the country, visit the Paris zoo or simply enjoy being together at home.

Sharing a few moments of tenderness, Françoise watches as Jean cuddles Julie after roughhousing in the country.

Jean and Françoise entertain by having people over on weekends in Paris. Here they joke during a card game with a journalist friend.

The family takes a stroll down a country lane on a damp Sunday afternoon. Jean and Françoise, in line with their own marital experience, have raised their girls to be independent and to ignore the restraints of traditional women's roles.

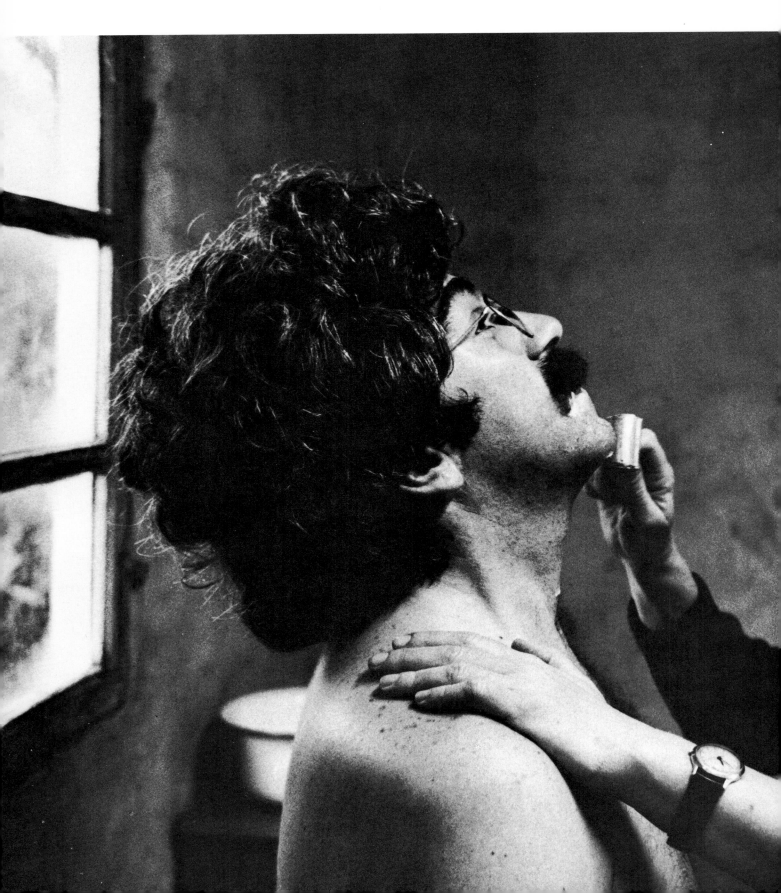

Jean keeps his chin up as Françoise shaves him in a ritual that few men would hold still for. In their new relationship, Françoise came to believe she was a better wife and mother because of her outside activities. Jean's doubts lingered—at home, he remarked, she sometimes seemed "present without really being present." And yet both agreed they had achieved an accommodation that worked: a marriage in which husband and wife were fully equal partners, in the new style, while preserving the warmth and comfort of the old-fashioned family.

Bibliography

Ardrey, Robert, *African Genesis*. Atheneum, 1967.

Asimov, Isaac, *The Human Body*. Houghton Mifflin Co., 1963.

Bardwick, Judith M., *Psychology of Women*. Harper & Row, Publishers, 1971.

Beals, Ralph L., and Harry Hoijer, *An Introduction to Anthropology*, 4th ed. The Macmillan Co., 1971.

Beauvoir, Simone de, *The Second Sex*. Modern Library, 1968.

Brecher, Edward M., *The Sex Researchers*. Little, Brown & Co., 1969.

Brenner, Charles, *An Elementary Textbook of Psychoanalysis*. International Universities Press, 1969.

Brittain, Vera, *Lady into Woman*. The Macmillan Co., 1953.

Clapp, Jane, *Art Censorship*. The Scarecrow Press, 1972.

Corson, Richard, *Fashions in Makeup*. Universe Books, 1972.

De Rachewiltz, Boris, *Black Eros*. Lyle Stuart, 1964.

Dublin, Louis I., *Factbook on Man*. The Macmillan Co., 1965.

Ellis, Havelock, *Man and Woman*. The Walter Scott Publishing Co., 1917.

Freud, Sigmund, *Collected Papers*, Vols. 1-5, James Strachey, ed. Basic Books, 1959.

Glazer-Malbin, Nona, and Helen Y. Waehrer, eds., *Woman In a Man-Made World*. Rand McNally & Co., 1973.

Hunt, Morton M.:
The Natural History of Love. Alfred A. Knopf, 1959.
Sexual Behavior in the 1970s. Playboy Press, 1974.

Kagan, Jerome, *Change and Continuity in Infancy*. John Wiley & Sons, 1971.

Karlen, Arno, *Sexuality and Homosexuality*. W. W. Norton & Co., 1971.

Kinsey, Alfred C.:
Sexual Behavior in the Human Female. W. B. Saunders Co., 1953.
Sexual Behavior in the Human Male. W. B. Saunders Co., 1948.

Komarovsky, Mirra, *Women in the Modern World*. Little, Brown & Co., 1953.

La Barre, Weston, *The Human Animal*. The University of Chicago Press, 1960.

Lidz, Theodore, *The Person*. Basic Books, 1968.

Maccoby, Eleanor, ed., *The Development of Sex Differences*. Stanford University Press, 1966.

Maccoby, Eleanor, and Carol N. Jacklin, *The Psychology of Sex Differences*. Stanford University Press, 1974.

Maisel, Albert, *The Hormone Quest*. Random House, 1965.

Marshall, Donald, and Robert Suggs, eds., *Human Sexual Behavior*. Basic Books, 1971.

Masters, William H., and Virginia E. Johnson:
Human Sexual Inadequacy. Little, Brown & Co., 1970.
Human Sexual Response. Little, Brown & Co., 1966.

Mead, Margaret:
Male and Female. William Morrow & Co., 1949.
Sex and Temperament in Three Primitive Societies. William Morrow & Co., 1935.

Michelmore, Susan, *Sexual Reproduction*. The Natural History Press, 1965.

Money, John, and Anke A. Ehrhardt, *Man & Woman, Boy & Girl*. The Johns Hopkins University Press, 1972.

Montagu, Ashley, *The Natural Superiority of Women*. The Macmillan Co., 1971.

Patai, Raphael, ed., *Women in the Modern World*. The Free Press, 1967.

Roazen, Paul, *Freud: Political and Social Thought*. Alfred A. Knopf, 1968.

Rosaldo, Michelle Zimbalist, and Louise Lamphere, eds., *Woman, Culture, and Society*. Stanford University Press, 1974.

Scheinfeld, Amram, *The Basic Facts of Human Heredity*. Washington Square Press, 1961.

Stoller, Robert J., *Sex and Gender*. Jason Aronson, 1974.

Strathern, Andrew and Marilyn, *Self-decoration in Mount Hagen*. University of Toronto Press, 1971.

Sullerot, Evelyne, *Woman, Society and Change*. World University Library, 1973.

Van Riper, Charles, *The Nature of Stuttering*. Prentice-Hall, 1971.

Zeldin, Theodore, *France, 1848-1945*. Oxford University Press, 1973.

Zubin, Joseph, and John Money, eds., *Contemporary Sexual Behavior: Critical Issues in the 1970s*. The Johns Hopkins University Press, 1973.

Picture Credits

Sem Presser. 51—Top, United Press International; Wide World—Middle, United Press International—Bottom, Wide World (2); United Press International. 52—Bill Ray from TIME-LIFE Picture Agency. 55 through 58—Elliott Erwitt from Magnum. 60—Anthony Barboza. 61 —Herbert Rogge. 62—Howard Sochurek from TIME-LIFE Picture Agency. 64—Esther Bubley. 66—Suzanne Szasz. 68—Dan Weiner. 73—Ken Heyman. 74—Peter Angelo Simon. 76—Howard Sochurek from Woodfin Camp and Associates. 78—Tony Ray-Jones, copyright © Anna Ray-Jones. 81—Lucien Clergue—Steven Salmieri. 82,83—René Burri from Magnum; Hank Walker from TIME-LIFE Picture Agency; Chester Higgins Jr. from Rapho Guillumette—Leonard Freed from Magnum. 85 —Norman Snyder. 86,87—Jacques-Henri Lartigue. 90—John Smart and John Wehrheim from Woodfin Camp and Associates. 92—Marc Riboud from Magnum. 94,95—Al Satterwhite. 96,97—Bass Charrington Ltd.; Courtesy Mellin S.p.A. Carnate, Milan; Imperial Tobacco Ltd.; Taken from the magazine I.P., Festival-73 of Spanish Creativity (July-August 1974)—Courtesy Nina Ricci, Paris; Firma Pfanni, Munich; Leo de Wys Inc.; Courtesy Philip Morris Inc. 98—Leonard McCombe from TIME-LIFE Picture Agency; No credit—Culver Pictures. 99—Culver Pictures—No credit; National Film Archive, copyright © Cinema International Corporation, U.K. 100—Courtesy F. Englisch GmbH, from their book Märchen; Courtesy Franklin Publications, Inc.—Ladybird Books Ltd., Loughborough, U.K.;

Courtesy Antonio Vallardi Editore, Milan; Cover from I, The Jury by Mickey Spillane, copyright © 1948 Mickey Spillane, reprinted by arrangement with The New American Library, Inc., New York, N.Y. 101—The Bettmann Archive; Gene Laurents—Luc Orient, "The Sixth Continent," E. Paape/Greg, Journal TINTIN. 102—Gene Laurents, courtesy Spelling-Goldberg Production, from The Rookies, Gerald S. O'Loughlin as Lt. Ryker; Friedhelm von Estorff, courtesy NDR, Hamburg, from The Incorrigibles and Love, featuring from left to right Monika Peitsch, Gernoth Endemann, Inge Meysel, Joseph Offenbach—Fuji TV—David Gahr, courtesy 20th Century-Fox. 103 —Courtesy CBS Inc—Giornalfoto, Milan. 104—Ikko. 108—Frank Lerner from TIME-LIFE Picture Agency; Giraudon, courtesy Musée Rodin. 109—The Metropolitan Museum of Art, Purchase Mr. and Mrs. William Coxe Gift, 1957—Scala, courtesy Musée du Louvre. 112—Helen Brush, Los Angeles Daily News. 115—The Bettmann Archive. 116,117—Gina Lollobrigida, from Italia Mia, published by Amphoto, Garden City, New York. 118 —Robert Doisneau from Rapho Guillumette. 122—© Arnold Newman. 123 —Paul Ockrassa. 124—Jean-Gil. 127 —United Press International. 130,131 —Claudia Andujar from Rapho Guillumette. 132—Roland and Sabrina Michaud from Rapho Guillumette. 133—Robert Lebeck from Black Star—Arthur Elgort, copyright © 1972 by The Condé Nast Publications Inc.; Douglas Faulkner. 134 —Loren McIntyre from Woodfin Camp

and Associates; Kay Lawson from Rapho Guillumette; Malcolm Kirk—Jay Maisel. 135—Douglas Faulkner—Klaus Paysan; Malcolm Kirk—Claudia Andujar from Rapho Guillumette; Carlo Mauri-Marka. 136—Elliott Erwitt from Magnum—Jay Maisel; Roland and Sabrina Michaud from Rapho Guillumette. 137—Roland Michaud from Rapho Guillumette. 138, 139—Eliot Elisofon, courtesy Eliot Elisofon estate; Yale Joel from TIME-LIFE Picture Agency. 140—Anders Engman. 144—Kay Lawson from Rapho Guillumette. 146—Marc and Evelyne Bernheim from Woodfin Camp and Associates. 148, 149—United Press International. 150,151 —Al Freni. 154,155—Row 1, left to right, United Press International; DPA; Perry Kretz, Stern; United Press International; Rick Solberg; Wide World; Arthur Siegel; Paul Stromski—Row 2, left to right, Peeter Vilms from Jeroboam; DPA; Thomas Höpker from Woodfin Camp and Associates; Wide World; Copyright Paul Almasy; United Press International (2); Leonard McCombe from TIME-LIFE Picture Agency—Row 3, left to right, Novosti from Sovfoto; Keystone; Photoreporters; Tass from Sovfoto; Harvey Stein; Wide World; Keystone; Abigail Heyman —Row 4, left to right, J. R. Eyerman from TIME-LIFE Picture Agency; Wide World; Dirk Reinartz, Stern; Dan McCoy from Black Star; DPA; Photoreporters; DPA; Jay Ullal, Stern. 157—Peeter Vilms from Jeroboam. 158,159—Jerry and Paul Koyce. 161—United Press International. 162 through 171—Richard Kalvar/VIVA from Woodfin Camp and Associates.

Acknowledgments

The author and editors of this book wish to thank the following persons and institutions for their assistance: Ruth Beasley, Coordinator, Information Service, Institute for Sex Relations, Indiana University, Bloomington; Mary Bodel, Office of Career Planning, Vassar College, Poughkeepsie, New York; W. Keith Daugherty, General Director, Family Service Association of America, New York City; Nancy Foner, Assistant Professor of Anthropology, State University of New York at Purchase; Alexander Grinstein, M.D., Detroit, Michigan; Jo Jacobs, Committee to Study Sex Discrimination in the Kalamazoo Public Schools, Kalamazoo, Michigan; Suzanne J. Kessler, Assistant Professor of Psychology, State University of New York at Purchase; Mirra Komarovsky, Professor of Sociology, Barnard College, New York City; Wendy McKenna, Research Assistant in Psychology, Graduate Center, City University of New York; John Money, Professor of Medical Psychology, Johns Hopkins University, Baltimore, Maryland; Susan Roberts, Public Relations Director, Family Service Association of America, New York City; William Selleck, Edina, Minnesota; Zelda Suplee, The Erickson Educational Foundation, New York City; Bluma Swerdloff, Associate Clinical Professor of Psychiatry, Psychoanalytic Clinic, Columbia University, New York City.

Index

✗ Printed in U.S.A.